Fred Zinnemann

Fred Zinnemann

Films of Character and Conscience

NEIL SINYARD

McFarland & Company, Inc., Publishers
Jefferson, North Carolina, and London

LIBRARY OF CONGRESS CATALOGUING-IN-PUBLICATION DATA

Sinyard, Neil.
  Fred Zinnemann : films of character and conscience /
Neil Sinyard.
      p.   cm.
  Includes bibliographical references and index.

  ISBN-13: 978-0-7864-1711-7
  (softcover : 50# alkaline paper) ∞

  1. Zinnemann, Fred, 1907–[1997] —Criticism and interpretation.
I. Title.
PN1998.3.Z56S56   2003
791.43'0233'092—dc21   2003014387

British Library cataloguing data are available

©2003 Neil Sinyard. All rights reserved

No part of this book may be reproduced or transmitted in any form or by any means, electronic or mechanical, including photocopying or recording, or by any information storage and retrieval system, without permission in writing from the publisher.

On the cover: Fred Zinnemann on location in the Swiss Alps during the filming of *Five Days One Summer* (1982).

Manufactured in the United States of America

McFarland & Company, Inc., Publishers
  Box 611, Jefferson, North Carolina 28640
    www.mcfarlandpub.com

Acknowledgments

Many people helped in the writing of this book. Fred Zinnemann's courteous collaboration was an invaluable asset. Gary Kurtz, Lucie Martin and Stanley Bielecki were a vital part of the initial production team, and without their help the book could not have been written.

For help with screenings of Zinnemann films, the assistance of Elaine Burrows of the National Film Archive, London, and Philip Strick of Harris Films was appreciable. I was especially indebted to Adrian Turner of the National Film Theatre in London and Mike Wachter of MGM/UA Entertainment in Los Angeles for arranging screenings of Mr. Zinnemann's shorts and early features.

For the opportunity to consult their unpublished interviews with Mr. Zinnemann, I acknowledge with gratitude the kindness of Bruce Norman and David Shipman. I would also like to acknowledge those critics whose writings on Zinnemann's films most stimulated me: Louis D. Giannetti, Gordon Gow, Gene D. Phillips, Alan Stanbrook, Andrew Sarris, Pauline Kael and Arthur Nolletti.

In the course of the research, I had the opportunity and good fortune to converse or correspond with a number of friends and collaborators of Mr. Zinnemann. The following were particularly generous with their time and help: writer Robert Anderson; director Alain Bonnot; writer and film historian Kevin Brownlow; writer Jon Cleary; production supervisor Terence Clegg; choreographer Agnes DeMille; actor Tony Franciosa; makeup artist George Frost; actress Julie Harris; actress Dame Wendy Hiller; actor Errol John; producer-director Stanley Kramer; actor Burt Lancaster; writer-director Joseph L. Mankiewicz; production executive Paul Mills; production manager Andrew Mitchell; writer Stewart Stern; writer Daniel Taradash; cinematographer Jean Tournier; and editor Elmo Williams.

During the major part of the writing, my wife Lesley offered indispensable support, administrative, critical and emotional. More recently, I have been deeply indebted to Sylvia Tynan for her expert secretarial skill in bringing this manuscript up to date.

For reasons indicated in the conclusion, I always regarded my work on Fred Zinnemann as unfinished business. I have never faltered in my admiration for the man and for his achievements as a filmmaker, and I am enormously grateful now for the opportunity to express that admiration in the way I always wanted: through a close analysis of some exceptional and imperishable films.

Contents

Acknowledgments	v
Introduction: The Man and the Movies	1
One. A Worm's Eye View of Hollywood, 1929–1948	9
Two. The Aftermath of War	31
Three. Character Is Destiny	61
Four. Variations on a Theme	99
Five. State of Terror	123
Six. Maidens and Mountains	151
Conclusion: The Quiet Master	161
Filmography	171
Appendix: Awards	179
Select Bibliography	183
Index	187

Introduction: The Man and the Movies

> Art is reality seen through a temperament.
> —Goethe

> A personal movie from a fool is far less interesting to me than a narrative movie from Fred Zinnemann. I would much rather watch Fred Zinnemann do one of his brilliant, craftsmanlike, sometimes inspired story-telling films than a personal blowing-up of someone who has nothing to say. And from his "narrative" movies, I actually know a great deal about Zinnemann.
> —Sidney Lumet

At the instigation of *Star Wars* producer Gary Kurtz, I first met Fred Zinnemann in the spring of 1982, when he was putting the finishing touches to what was to prove his last film, *Five Days One Summer*. Over the next two years, I interviewed him on many occasions in his Mayfair offices in London, with a view to writing an authorized biography. The project did not work out. The most private of men, Zinnemann instinctively resisted the idea of telling his life story except in terms so limited as to be frustrating to any biographer wanting to dig a little beneath the surface. In fairness, I should say that I found myself becoming less drawn to the idea of biography and more towards the idea of a critical appreciation of the films. I was, in fact, coming to the same conclusion on Zinnemann as Sidney Lumet in the epigraph above—namely, that the films revealed more about Zinnemann than the man himself was prepared to disclose. Zinnemann published a lavishly illustrated but personally reticent autobiography in 1992, five years before his death. Since then, apart from a fine volume of essays edited by Arthur Nolletti Jr. in 1999 (see bibliography), in critical terms Zinnemann has remained a curiously neglected figure. Hence this book.

To any objective and informed observer, the neglect of Zinnemann must seem a massive omission in film literature. There is no other monograph on him to the best of my knowledge; there are few adequate critical accounts of some of his most famous films such as *The Nun's Story* (1959) and *A Man for All Seasons* (1966). Yet Zinnemann was one of the most honored and respected film-makers in the world, establishing his reputation with early films like *The Seventh Cross* (1944) and *The Search* (1948) and consolidating it with the acknowledged classics *High Noon* (1952), *From Here to Eternity* (1953) and *Julia* (1977). He not only worked with some of the biggest stars of the screen (Marlon Brando, Montgomery Clift, Spencer Tracy, Gary Cooper, Robert Mitchum, Audrey Hepburn, Jane Fonda, among others), in some cases it was he who first introduced them to film audiences. He was one of the rare directors who could attract a star to a project on the basis of his name alone. "That's what I came for!" says Sean Connery's character in *Five Days One Summer* (1982) when he sees the fateful mountain: Connery acknowledges that what he came for as an actor was the association with Fred Zinnemann. Over four decades, Zinneman raised the level of intelligence of popular cinema, always treating the audience as adults, never treating film simply as product. His name on the credits meant a particular kind of thoughtful, quality filmmaking. He was that rare thing: a filmmakers' film-maker whose pictures communicate and succeed on their own terms with mass audiences.

Although he enjoyed the memoirs of other directors (he was a great admirer of John Huston's *An Open Book*), he never encouraged the idea of a book being written about himself or his work.

Introduction

"The early period in Hollywood is interesting, because of my worm's eye perspective," he told me, "but after that it's just another more or less boring success story." For further clarification, he would say, "I don't like looking back," but one sensed something more: the reserve of an intensely private man who did not want a certain area of himself invaded. Like the man, his films spoke quietly. He lived in London for the last 30 years or so, finding privacy still just about possible and England a "congenial" country in which to live. By contrast, he must have cut an unorthodox figure in Hollywood when he lived there. His quiet, reserved demeanor was quite at variance with the flamboyance of the film capital in its heyday. But then the films he was to make went against the grain of the action and exuberance associated with the American cinema. This difference is attributable to Zinnemann's own personality and preferences, but also to his European eye, which assessed the heroic male of Hollywood stereotype with a quizzical irony. "I don't care about the fact that a man is shooting a gun," he said to me. "What I want to know is *why* he is shooting it."

Fred Zinnemann was born in Vienna in 1907, the elder son of Dr. Oskar and Anna Zinnemann. He could be described as belonging to what one might call the Second Viennese School of Hollywood filmmaking, the legacy of the older Austro-German generation of Stroheim, Lang, Murnau, Pabst, Lubitsch and Ophuls being bequeathed to directors such as Wilder, Preminger, Siodmak and Zinnemann. Of these, there is no question that Fred Zinnemann was the least flashy, the most sober and self-effacing. There was none of the opulent decadence or delirious dementia of some of his fellow emigrés, and little of their Expressionist extremes. This is not to say that the Viennese was an unimportant element of the Zinnemann character. To meet him was to be reminded of an Old World courtesy that one encounters rarely today. But the Viennese element expressed itself somewhat differently in his films.

Zinnemann's most vivid memories of Vienna, he told me, were of those formative years immediately after the Great War, and the memories of malnutrition and children's diseases caused by the Allied blockade and by the economic shortages. Such recollections must have influenced and darkened his outlook. His films are obsessed by war and societies in a visible process of disintegration. Taken together, they comprise a partial history of the turbulent politics of the twentieth century, at different times surveying the consequences of the Spanish Civil War, the traumatic impact of World War II, and the ravages of McCarthyism in America. The claustrophobia and cultural conservatism of Vienna certainly contributed to his passionate desire to leave Central Europe and to the huge impact of Hollywood on him when he first arrived. His first-hand experience of Vienna's notorious anti–Semitism was reflected in his films in his insistence on human dignity and in his fascination with the outsider who feels at odds with the society to which he ostensibly belongs.

Gustav Mahler once said, "I am thrice homeless—as a native of Bohemia in Austria, as an Austrian amongst Germans, and as a Jew throughout the world." At various stages throughout his life, Fred Zinnemann must have felt similarly "thrice homeless." He was very aware of being a Jew in Vienna. He sometimes felt like a foreigner in Hollywood; when *The Search* attained success, some in Hollywood regarded Zinnemann as a "newly arrived" Swiss director, despite the fact that he had been living and working in America for nearly 20 years. He was occasionally made to feel a Hollywood director in Britain, expressing to me, for example, his delight at the Oscar success of *Chariots of Fire* (1981) but his surprise by the omission in the press and elsewhere of *A Man for All Seasons* in the list of previous British winners. All of this must have had an impact on a person of his hypersensitivity. Success did not seem to make him any more secure or complacent or relaxed. He once told me he had a massive inferiority complex. He still had crises of self-confidence that were, however, compensated for by a ferocious will.

Such perplexities of personality arise from a variety of causes. "Outwardly," writer Stewart Stern told me, "he seemed perfectly controlled, but inwardly one sensed a tremendous volatility." (One has the same sense from some of his films of simmering emotions under a disciplined surface.) I never heard Fred Zinnemann raise his voice, nor saw his anger, but I have been told by people who knew him well that the signs were unmistakable (a frown of the eyebrows, the eyes turning a metallic blue, a white bar on his forehead visible beneath the skin) and that when they showed, a person who knew what was good for him better back up immediately. Overstepping the mark at rehearsal session of *From Here to Eternity*, Burt Lancaster was told quietly but firmly by Zinnemann that his contract indicated that *he* was the director of this movie, and not Lancaster. Zinnemann did not lose his temper, he *used* it. Generally, the reason was that there was a production battle that he needed to win. The refusal to compromise, undoubtedly nurtured by his bruising early experiences with MGM, resulted in a determination to keep artistic control that in turn led to finer but fewer films. "There are directors who would just have taken the money and run," said the producer Gary Kurtz, who knew him well, "but Fred Zinnemann was not one of those."

There was in Zinnemann an intriguing combination of softness and steel. He was gentle with actors, leading them patiently in a direction which he felt was the right way to go but at the same time wanting them to feel that they had found the route themselves, so that the destination was arrived at through collaboration, not coercion. His films treated audiences in the same way. He had a strong conviction about the material he directed but he left room for an audience to make up its own mind about what it sees. At the same time, to achieve what he wanted, he could—to borrow Robert Bolt's phrase about Thomas More in *A Man for All Seasons*—"set like metal and be no more budged than a cliff." "He could be very stubborn," Daniel Taradash told me, adding, "Mind you—he was nearly always right."

"He knew precisely what he wanted and would not let anything come against it," said assistant director Alain Bonnot, who observed Zinnemann at close quarters and had a deep affection and admiration for the man. This will is one of the reasons that working for him was simultaneously a challenge, a joy and a nightmare. He was extremely difficult to satisfy and seemingly indefatigable in his pursuit of perfection. I once mentioned to him his reputation as a "perfectionist." He bridled somewhat at the word, but by the time he had finished kicking it around—pondering whether the word was synonymous with pedantry, prodding it suspiciously from all sides, satisfying himself that he had fully considered its implications—I thought the point seemed to have been confirmed.

There were at least three enormously significant occasions in Zinnemann's life when that will was severely tested and did not wilt in the face of great pressure. There was his defiance of his family in his determination to become a filmmaker in 1927; his decision in the mid–1940s to opt for suspension by MGM in preference to shooting another of their B-picture scripts; and his action in taking legal proceedings against MGM in 1969 after their cancellation of *Man's Fate* only a few days before it was due to start shooting. There was also his principled resistance to the McCarthyist hysteria of the early 1950s (which is more fully dealt with in the section on *High Noon*). Each occasion called on the utmost reserves of conviction and inner strength. The most striking thing about these occasions perhaps is the reminder they give of the stands taken by the leading characters in the most famous of Zinnemann's films: the Marshal in *High Noon*, Prewitt in *From Here to Eternity*, Sister Luke in *The Nun's Story*, Sir Thomas More in *A Man for All Seasons*. All of these stands are taken alone (and Zinnemann would describe himself as a "loner"), and it is significant in this regard that his most successful films—one might add *Julia* to the above—are those which concentrate substantially on a single individual. This might be the reason that, when the structure is more diffuse, the films sometimes lack focus and drama. It might also explain why a director like him would stand out now against a more impersonal contemporary cinema that seems often to be the province of lawyers, financiers and computers, and to lack the passion and flair of the showmen of the past.

The essence of this individualist position was best expressed, according to Zinnemann, by Hillel around 2,000 years ago: "If I am not for myself, who will be for me? And if I am for myself alone, what then am I? And if not now, when?" His films examined solitary stands of principle against a community or institution willing the individual to forget his conscience and compromise and conform. The narratives can be read as interrupted and uncertain journeys towards self-realization, a journey which often involves the crossing of physical and psychological borders, but a destination Henrik Ibsen has described as "the highest goal man can attain."

This pervasive theme is, one might think, especially relevant to the situation of a professional and an artist seeking personal expression in an industry devoted to commerce. Yet Zinnemann's memories of participating in the Hollywood studio system at the height of its popularity became very positive ones. He looked back with admiration on the kind of studio efficiency and teamwork which enabled, for example, a film as complicated as *From Here to Eternity* to be shot within six weeks. He reflected appreciatively on the way the studios nurtured young stars, and on the fervor and showmanship of the "founding fathers" of the industry who ate, slept and dreamt films (a spirit embodied by the famous Goldwynism: "I don't care if this film doesn't make a nickel, but I want everybody in America to see it!"). Above all, he was grateful. "I was thrilled to be there when I first arrived in Hollywood in 1929," he told me. "It was a grand adventure in those days and I had come with great hopes which in the event were more than fulfilled. Where else could I possibly have had such chances as came my way?"

The early part of the book deals with Zinnemann's struggle to attain a position whereby he could make films of his own choice and in his own way, until the breakthrough with *The Search*. Thereafter the films are grouped, with very little violence to chronology, according to major themes: the ravages of war, the "sovereignty of selfhood" (Dennis Potter's phrase), character as destiny, the outsider in society, politics and the liberal conscience. The circumstances of the making of the films are integrated with a critical commentary on the films themselves. They include comments from the director and fellow collaborators, who expressed to me their gratitude for their association with Zinnemann and for the fights he frequently fought on their behalf. (Unless otherwise indicated, all direct quotations in the text are taken from conversations or correspondence with the author.) Fred Zinnemann's story is the evolution of an outstanding filmmaker and a fascinating man. A new book on his career is timely. If not now, when?

CHAPTER ONE

A Worm's Eye View of Hollywood, 1929–1948

From Vienna to America

When Fred Zinnemann discovered he did not have the talent to be a musician and that his bachelor's degree in law at the University of Vienna had been obtained at the cost of massive boredom, he turned his attention to the cinema. Four films he saw, instead of attending lectures, were to change his life. They were Erich von Stroheim's *Greed* (1923), Sergei Eisenstein's *Battleship Potemkin* (1925), King Vidor's *The Big Parade* (1925) and Carl Dreyer's *The Passion of Joan of Arc* (1928). Why did they have such influence? They were all films in a particular mode of social realism, and this was to be the kind of stylistic path Zinnemann was to follow. They were films that illustrated the visual, emotional and creative potential of the new medium. Above all, they gave the young man a sense of the cinema's enormous potential for self-expression. "They gave me the certainty that it was the director who really created the picture."

There were no theatrical traditions in his family. Indeed, in the Vienna of the Twenties, there was a great gap between the mostly conservative and tradition-bound professional class and film people, who were definitely not regarded as solid citizens. When he told his family of his ambition, there was consternation that did not subside until the persistence of the young man began to impress them. "I was besieged by groups of uncles and aunts who had been hurriedly sent for to help change my mind and who would come at me two or three at a time. It was thought that working in films was, quite obviously, not a serious occupation and that I was being led astray by visions of glamour and pretty girls. Finally, my father intervened and the family relented when they saw I had dug in my heels. But they insisted, quite rightly, that if this was what I wanted, I should be properly trained."

At the age of 20 in 1927, he followed a schoolfriend, Gunter von Fritsch, to the newly founded Technical School for Cinematography in Paris. Here he learned the fundamentals of optics, developing and printing the negative, photo-chemistry, even projection, and worked with fairly ancient silent cameras. Unable to obtain work in France because he was not a French citizen, he left Paris with some sadness and moved to Berlin where he found jobs on three films. One of them, *Ich Kusse Ihre Hand, Madame,* featured an early screen appearance from Marlene Dietrich. The best known of these films was *Menschen am Sonntag* (1929), directed by Robert Siodmak, assisted by Edgar Ulmer and written by Billy Wilder. Zinnemann was assistant to the cameraman Eugene Shufftan (later to do distinguished work in Hollywood and win an Oscar for *The Hustler*). It was a tiny film, shot entirely on location, and none of the young hopefuls who made it had any idea that a little piece of screen history was being made and that all of their careers were pointing in the direction of Hollywood.

Early Days in Hollywood

When sound came to the movies and *The Jazz Singer* (1927) was all the rage, film production in Berlin temporarily came to a complete halt. Zinnemann thought that it would be a smart move to go to America and learn all he could about the new invention before returning to Europe. He arrived in New York in October

1929 after a six-day boat trip from Cherbourg, with just three assets: a basic knowledge of the English language; the large sum of $500 from his father; and a letter of introduction to the head of Universal Studios, Carl Laemmle (known as "Uncle Carl"), famous for his patronage of aspiring young talents. Laemmle had nothing special in mind for the young Zinnemann but he passed him over to a casting director who quickly got rid of him by making him an extra for a film then shooting at Universal, Lewis Milestone's classic anti-war drama *All Quiet on the Western Front* (1930). Zinnemann became a German soldier and also doubled as a French ambulance driver. Six weeks' hard work was abruptly terminated when he was fired for answering back to an assistant director. "I wasn't a rebel: I just didn't like being pushed around."

An important contact in his early years was the famous Berlin stage director, Berthold Viertel, who had come to Hollywood to write films for F.W. Murnau and was now making films at Fox. After being fired from *All Quiet on the Western Front*, Zinnemann landed the job of assisting Viertel. The professional contact lasted intermittently between 1931 and 1934. Zinnemann by that time was technically well-prepared, knowing as much as any operating cameraman. He learned from Viertel how to work with actors and how to organize a scene. He saw how a big studio operated, the way in which a production was lined up and what happened after it was finished, all invaluable practical knowledge. Becoming his assistant, friend and linguistic helpmate, he also became included in Viertel's distinguished circle of friends. It was through Viertel that he met the man who was to be the greatest artistic influence on his career, Robert Flaherty.

Robert Flaherty

"I knew him by reputation, of course, as the maker of *Nanook of the North*, and the 'father of documentary' before the word had really been heard of," Zinnemann said. Flaherty was in Hollywood at this time, having come back from the South Seas after making *Tabu* with Murnau, which had not been a very happy experience. Meeting him at Viertel's house and knowing he was planning to make a film in Europe, Zinnemann asked if he could assist him. "If you can get to Berlin under your own steam, you can," replied Flaherty. Which is what he did, discovering that Flaherty was negotiating with the Soviet Trade Mission in Berlin for permission to make a film about a remote tribe in the Soviet part of Central Asia on the actual location. The film eventually fell through, in Zinnemann's view, because the two parties could not agree on its subject. Flaherty wanted, characteristically, a poetic monument to a way of life that had escaped modern civilization but was fast disappearing. The Soviets wanted a propagandist film showing how much better the life of these nomads was after the Revolution. In the end, Flaherty ran out of money and went to Ireland to make *Man of Aran* (1933). Zinnemann returned to Hollywood, having had his first experience of something that was to happen to him a lot in his later career: preparing for a film which was ultimately not made. Like Flaherty, Zinnemann always preferred to withdraw from rather than compromise with a film if it could not be made according to certain standards which, in his view, alone would make it work. *The Old Man and the Sea*, *Hawaii* and *The French Lieutenant's Woman* were only some of the future projects Zinnemann subsequently felt compelled to leave because of this.

Zinnemann's working experience with Flaherty consisted of little more than camera tests and guidance on the use of lenses, but he was considerably influenced by Flaherty's views on filmmaking. It was Flaherty who had really shown that documentary need not be synonymous with advertizing or educational films, or boredom. That influence shines through the early shorts Zinnemann made for MGM, which tried to create drama and human interest as well as simply relay information. As Flaherty did, Zinnemann liked to spend a long time with the subjects of his films, researching, talking to the people, getting to know the rhythm of life of a community before committing it to film. Films as far apart as *The Wave*, *The Search* and *The Nun's Story* all have that specific element of Flaherty influence in them and benefit enormously from it. Like Flaherty, he always preferred being outdoors on actual locations. Like his mentor, he enjoyed working with non-actors.

"In fact, originally I wanted to be a documentary director," Zinnemann recalled. "My idea of happiness was to be on an expedition making films about adventurous places." At that time, though, documentary films were few and far between, and Hollywood's definition of a documentary film was immortalized by the president of Columbia Pictures, Harry Cohn: "A documentary is a picture without women. If there's one woman in it, it's a semi-documentary." Nevertheless, the documentary inclination in Fred Zinnemann was never subdued. It is no coincidence that his first big critical success, *The Search*, was the first film in which MGM gave him the freedom to shoot on the actual locations of the story, which was so essential to the film's force and conviction. Authenticity of location in *The Nun's Story* and *Five Days One Summer* contributed also to the authenticity of the performances, where the actors were compelled to live the lives, in some respects, of the characters they were playing. There is a minimum of fakery in the films, in other words, which becomes a thematic *leitmotif* as well.

If Flaherty influenced him greatly as a filmmaker, he influenced him even more as a man. Zinnemann met Flaherty at an impressionable age, so he was undoubtedly all the more struck by the latter's appearance, his wit, his conviviality, his friendship and that typically perverse streak of Irish humour that led Flaherty for some time afterwards to refer to Fred mischievously as the worst assistant he had ever had. But beyond that was Flaherty's independence of spirit.

"Flaherty was totally his own man, not for one second thinking of any sort of compromise, professional or otherwise," Zinnemann stated. Flaherty's disregard of financial reward put him at odds with the Hollywood system. He never sought anything less than perfection, and one of the consequences for him as a filmmaker was a relatively small body of work. There are parallels with Zinnemann's own career here. Flaherty's battles with the MGM hierarchy at the end of the 1920s (walking off his assignment on *The White Shadows in the South Seas* when he saw the appalling behavior of Hollywood actors in Tahiti and then insulting L.B. Mayer when the latter tried to dissuade him) seem to foreshadow Zinnemann's own problems in the mid–1940s. Like Flaherty, Zinnemann's increasing stature and power as a filmmaker paradoxically made for a dwindling body of films, because of his insistence on making them on his own terms. Such a consideration gives a slightly different inflection to the films themselves. It is not simply that they examine the characteristics that interest him about human personality—behavior under stress, dignity, courage and cowardice. They are about the kind of individualism that can run into trouble in the film world. His recurrent theme of the individual in conflict with a large institution is, of course, relevant to the film industry itself. Zinnemann had glimpsed the nature of this struggle in Robert Flaherty. He was to recognize its importance during the difficult years when he was a contract director at MGM.

These early years in Hollywood had their difficulties and disappointments. The Depression was at its height and when he returned to America after his period with Flaherty, Zinnemann found it difficult to obtain jobs. At one stage he seriously planned a book of photographs on New York, a project finally felt to be too expensive at the time of the Depression by the publishing houses. Later, in 1932, he helped Gregg Toland and Busby Berkeley select camera angles for the dance sequences from the Eddie Cantor vehicle, *The Kid from Spain* ("there wasn't much I could contribute that masters like Berkeley and Toland didn't know already"). It would be fair to say that, at this time, Zinnemann was appalled by the lack of imagination of most early American talkies, which seemed little more than third-rate photographed theater. The magic of the silent film had gone, which must have increased the young man's frustration and his determination to make some contribution of his own to the medium.

The Wave *(1934–1935)*

Zinnemann's directing debut came about indirectly through Flaherty. Through him, he met other documentary directors, including Henwar Rodakiewicz who was due to make a documentary in Mexico with the great photographer Paul Strand. Strand had been commissioned by composer-conductor Carlos Chavez (at that time head of the Mexican Department of Fine Art with overall responsibility for all cultural matters) to make a film about the life of fishermen that would alert Mexicans to the harsh plight of their fellow countrymen. When Rodakiewicz found that he had a previous commitment, he recommended Zinnemann instead.

The schedule called for four months' shooting to do *The Wave*, but it actually took a year. The team was based in a small town near the jungle where they were thrown very much on their own resources. It was physically hard, but a tremendously happy experience, because there was a lot of time to live with the people and absorb the atmosphere. Although the credits list a co-director, Gomez Muriel, Zinnemann directed: Muriel's role was that of an assistant director. (Rodakiewicz directed two brief sequences.) The film is about the exploitation of local fishermen in the tropics near Vera Cruz and the attempt of one of them to form them into a union, which results in his being killed. As an early contribution to the development of the Mexican cinema, a comment on conditions then in Central America, and as an intriguing and less ambitious precursor of Visconti's thematically similar *La Terra Trema* (1948), the film remains a fascinating document.

It is a finely crafted film, excellently edited by Gunter von Fritsch, and youthfully infused with a tone of anger, technical boldness and a clutch of cinematic influences, either conscious or accidental. The use of visual imagery as poetic metaphor continues the experimentation of Pudovkin in films like *Mother* (1926). The film's political fervor, its perfectly timed close-up of the clenched fist, derives from the "cinema-fist" technique of Eisenstein's *Battleship Potemkin*. *Potemkin* is also evoked in a menacing shot of the legs of soldiers as they approach to quell the workers' riots, bringing the specter of the Odessa steps to that Mexican beach. (It is worth recalling that, prior to *The Wave*, Eisenstein himself had an ill-fated attempt to make a film about Mexico, *Que Viva Mexico!*). The major influence is Flaherty, in the film's authentic reconstruction of the lives of people of a different culture, and in its imposing view of the relation between Man and Nature. The use of natural imagery (shadow, lowering sky) to emphasize the film's emotional coloring is to become one of the most characteristic of Zinnemann effects, temperature and climate echoing temperament and mood.

As a first film, one might see it also as a precursor of subsequent Fred Zinnemann trademarks, though it was to be a long time before he was to have the freedom to develop themes and setting to its full advantage. Technically, it establishes his preference for location filming and his roots in documentary. Thematically, it establishes the character of his social concerns and his sympathy for those who are willing to fight and even die to maintain dignity, self-respect and justice.

Short Films

Zinnemann started with MGM about a year after he had come back from Mexico. At that time he still had the ambition of becoming a documentary director but had found no regular work. He earned money during this time by co-authoring a screenplay with Henwar Rodakiewicz called *Bonanza* (1935) about a young Mexican Indian; it was sold to MGM for $3,000 but never produced. He also had a three-day stint as "technical adviser" on the William Wyler film, *These Three* (1936), supervising the dressing of a Vienna café set, and even daring to suggest a camera angle to the director. Wyler was speechless, then laughed, remembering that he had done the same thing when he was a message boy at Universal. "This fellow is going to be a film director some day," Wyler said. It was all part of the education of a young man on the bottom rung of the cinema ladder and, from this worm's eye perspective, learning how the industry worked. In 1937, discovering that MGM had a Short Subjects Department, which they used as a training ground for actors, writers and directors whom they thought had some promise, Zinnemann submitted a couple of reels from *The Wave* and, on the strength of that, he was accepted.

The Shorts Department was run by two men, Jack Chertok and his assistant, Richard Goldstone, who were responsible for the organization of the whole division. A director was given a choice of scripts that had been written by studio writers, and then had a reasonable time to prepare, work on a second draft, cast it, etc. The films were shot silent, with narration added later. The restrictions were those of money (a budget of $15,000 for one reel of film, a third of which went on overhead) and time (a shooting schedule of three days per reel).

You learned a tremendous amount from that: the discipline of being able to tell a story in ten minutes—the length of one reel—and how to organize a miniature production, so that you could shoot about 20 to 30 camera set-ups a day. You had to be one step ahead of everybody and know not only what you were doing but what you were going to do. If you wanted a crowd scene, you had to recognize that, on that budget, this meant ten people. You could never use a moving camera because it would take too long to light the set. There was no point in having a window or a piece of carpet in the set if you were not going to show them.

This training was enormously beneficial to Zinnemann in his later career. It gave him the experience of pre-visualizing a film, of retaining a clear sense of where the significant emphases are, even when shooting out of continuity. It taught him filmic discipline: The severe restrictions on time meant that problems were not there to complicate things but there as a challenge to be solved.

Zinnemann worked in the Department from 1937 to 1942. It was generally a happy and successful time, which prepared him for the transition from one-reelers to two-reelers on the *Crime Does Not Pay* series and for the ultimate transition to feature films. (It proved a similar training ground for excellent young directors such as Jules Dassin, George Sidney, David Miller and Roy Rowland.) His film *That Mothers Might Live*, about Dr. Semmelweis, a pioneer in the use of antiseptics in obstetrics, won an Oscar as the best short of 1938. Another short, *The Story of Dr. Carver* (1938), audaciously covered 90 years in ten minutes in telling of the life of a Negro, kidnapped by raiders when he was a baby, who became an eminent scientist. "I was proud of that film. Every shot was a miniature sequence in itself. But it was not only valuable technically. It was done at a time when blacks in films were trusted servants or happy slaves or largely objects of ridicule or caricature. To show a Negro as a man of dignity and not simply as crude comic relief was not usual then. A film like King Vidor's *Hallelujah* was a rare exception."

One would not look too closely at these films for indications of Zinnemann's future development. Although he had some measure of choice, the director in that situation was largely a hired hand, the main challenge being to realize the writer's ideas as clearly and as economically as possible. In Zinnemann's shorts, the subjects ranged from sleeping sickness (*Tracking the Sleeping Death*) to climatology (*Weather Wizards*), from a history of the American cotton industry (*The Old South*) to the funny things people request in their last will and testament (*Your Last Act*). The two subjects that recur most insistently are dogs and doctors. The medical motif in a lot of the shorts (*That Mothers Might Live, One Against the World, They Live Again*) fleetingly reminds one that Zinnemann's father was a physician. *Friend Indeed* (1938) and *Stuffie* (1940) are shaggy dog stories narrated by Pete Smith that might have had the unfortunate consequence of typecasting Zinnemann as Metro's animal director, judging from early feature assignments such as *Eyes in the Night* (1942) and *My Brother Talks to Horses* (1947).

Technically the films are assured and sometimes adventurous. A striking money montage, reminiscent of *Greed*, links the episodes of *Your Last Act* (1941). A freeze-frame is used for comic effect in *Stuffie*. An elaborate slow dissolve visually forges a link between the efforts of an eighteenth century pioneering engineer and the destruction of a First World War German submarine in *The Ash-Can Fleet* (1939). Southern mansions crumble in slow motion, to the sound of a lightning crack, in *The Old South* (1940). Fast montages, matching image and narration strikingly convey delirium and hysteria in *That Mothers Might Live* and *One Against the World* (1939). There is even a use of split-screen—doctors washing their hands/babies being born—to suggest Dr. Semmelweis's contribution to safe childbirth in *That Mothers Might Live*.

Thematically, a number of the films (*That Mothers Might Live, One Against the World, The Ash-Can Fleet, Forgotten Victory*) are about individuals who come into conflict with colleagues, institutions or society, and are forced into the roles of outsiders—certainly hints of things to come in his later work. "One Against the World" is a Fred Zinnemann title if ever there was one.

The last story, *The Lady or the Tiger?* (1942), is one of the most playful and intriguing. A barbaric ceremony in ancient times offers a variation on being sacrificed to the lions: the victim has to choose one of two doors to open, out of which will come either a lady, whom he must marry, or a tiger. One such lowly victim is about to be punished for having an affair with a princess. Endeavoring to save him, the princess has discovered the secret of the doors, but has also found out that the lady who will be behind one of the doors has been her lover's mistress. On the day of the ceremony, will the princess be guided by love or by jealousy? He looks towards her; she gives a sign; he opens one of the doors—and the film ends. In a way it is a very characteristic Zinnemann movie. It is all about the necessity and yet perilousness of choice. It ends, literally, in the way nearly all of his movies end metaphorically, on a question mark.

The two Zinnemann shorts for the *Crime Does Not Pay* series exemplify how the films of the period had to be sensitive to social and political change. *White America Sleeps* (1939) is about espionage and the infiltration of foreign spies into the industry of a nation, "whose sole intention," as the narration puts it, "is to remain at peace in a troubled world." The chief character, Dave Miller, photographs secret information for money. The action builds to a climax of double-cross and shoot-out and Miller, who is more stupid than evil, is led away in chains. The film ostensibly offers an isolationist stance because, as is well known, Hollywood was at this time very ambivalent and uneasy about committing itself to any sort of endorsement of war in Europe. At the same time, it carries an implicit criticism of American complacency about the European situation. The title brings to mind the final paragraph of George Orwell's *Homage to Catalonia*, when he returns from a war-torn Spain and talks of the "deep, deep sleep of England, from which I sometimes fear that we shall never wake till we are jerked out of it by the roar of bombs." It could be equally applicable to America before Pearl Harbor.

Forbidden Passage (1941) was made two years later and is a more committed and technically more assured film. Dedicated to the Immigration Service, the film is not a cautionary indictment of excessive immigration but of ruthless smugglers who are making money from desperate people fleeing from Hitler's Europe who have to wait to be allowed into the USA because of the quota system. Unusually for the *Crime Does Not Pay* series, the emphasis on human tragedy transcends any simple moralizing.

Early Films (1942–47)

When Jack Chertok was promoted from the Shorts Department to a producer of features, he took Fred Zinnemann with him, the latter signing a seven-year contract. It turned out to be one of the most frustrating periods of his career, offering a measure of financial security in return for the pressure of conformity.

He rapidly came up against some of the contradictions of the studio system. The technical expertise was second to none. But room for maneuver was severely restricted. Zinnemann looked with increasing admiration on giants like John Ford and George Stevens, who had fought for and won a measure of creative freedom.

According to Zinnemann, "There's the famous story when a trembling member of the production staff had to inform Ford that he was three days behind schedule. 'How many pages am I supposed to shoot a day?' Ford asked, gruffly. 'Four,' the man said. So Ford took the script, tore out 12 pages, handed them to the man and said: 'Right—I'm back on schedule.' George Stevens was another of our heroes in this respect. He was known as the man with the Indian look because he had a massive, impassive face and could at times look just like a stone monument. He was a painstaking worker and it was always said about George that, after two weeks shooting, he would probably be six weeks behind schedule. The producer would come running down, tearing his hair, practically sobbing, remonstrating with him for minutes on end. And George would just stare unblinkingly at him with that great doleful face. And when the man had spluttered to a halt, George would simply say, 'Thank you very much,' get up and walk away, and carry on as if nothing had happened. He just wore them down. Men like Ford and Stevens were an inspiration, but they had to fight hard to get into that position."

It was not easy to win such battles for artistic control at MGM, a studio run by a man, Louis B. Mayer, who insisted that his stars' close-ups should be brightly lit "even if it were midnight in a tunnel," and who put the director as the fourth important member of the production team (below the producer, the star and the script). There was little opportunity for the average young director to impose his own vision on the material. If he did, the studio bush telegraph would start spreading the word that he was "difficult," news that would also travel to other studios. At that juncture, his career would be in trouble.

To begin with, there was no hint of the trouble to come. Zinnemann's first feature film, *Kid Glove Killer* (1942), is a B-movie of some interest and skill. "It was a nice little script which at that time seemed to me very important, and I was delighted to have a chance to do a feature. We shot it in three weeks, with no trouble, because we were well-organized and I had the good fortune of having a fine cast. I liked working with Van Heflin very much. He had a modest estimate of himself and did not take himself or the profession too seriously. I'd been amused by his performance in *Johnny Eager* where he'd upstaged Robert Taylor by the simple expedient of blowing his nose through the star's lines!"

Kid Glove Killer is really *Crime Does Not Pay* with chemistry, about a corrupt local politician whose involvement with a racketeer is eventually exposed by clever police lab work. It has an air of competent nonchalance. Its view of city politicians and authority figures generally is breezily disrespectful. "Do I look like a mayor?" says the newly elected Mayor Daniels to his radio reporter friend, Gerry, who responds: "Not exactly, you look honest." (The remark is revealing about Gerry's duplicity: The Mayor's honesty is later to cost him his life when he threatens to reveal Gerry's association with the gangster and Gerry plants a bomb in his car.) The best visual joke of the film is Zinnemann's image of faceless bureaucracy: a shot of three identical chairbacks with smoke emanating from each as a voice tells Gerry (Lee Bowman) that he will be offered the mayorship if he solves the Mayor's murder.

The dramatic situation is intriguing: a man who has to investigate and prosecute for his own advancement a crime which he himself has committed. It is one of a number of details in the film which interestingly anticipates Billy Wilder's classic film noir, *Double Indemnity* (1944). Quite an interesting triangular relationship develops when Gerry (for ulterior motives) begins to take an interest in Miss Mitchell (assistant to the scientist, McKay) and McKay becomes unaccountably jealous. There is a lively scene in a restaurant between the three of them where their fluctuating relationship is signified by the way, in a quite natural sequence of events, they keep shifting chairs, alternating who sits next to the girl. For if Gerry is faced with a professional and personal dilemma, so too is McKay. His increasing conviction that Gerry is involved in the Mayor's murder is paralleled by his observation that Miss Mitchell is falling in love with Gerry. How can he solve the crime without breaking her heart? It is a typical crisis of conscience, heavily underlined when McKay turns up a message card that reads: "Once to every man and nation comes the moment to decide." As it happens, Miss Mitchell discovers Gerry's duplicity at almost the same time as McKay and justice is happily done.

The contrast between the character of McKay and Gerry is quite interesting. McKay has a habit of tossing a dart at a silhouette of the human body on his door and invariably missing. The impression he gives overall is of a man who keeps missing the target, a smart character who has not got all he might have out of life. Gerry, on the other hand, is not as bright, but he is pushy and aggressive, a man determined to get ahead and wield power. An ambitious, not so talented man is contrasted with a not-so-ambitious, slightly embittered, underrated professional. "My friend," McKay says ironically to his chief, "you're soured by too much contact with humanity." The film has fun with all the laboratory paraphernalia which permits McKay to investigate the crime through minute examination of keys, nails, specimens of hair and the like. What Zinnemann is seeking, however, is material which will allow him to put human nature itself under the microscope.

In contrast to *Kid Glove Killer*, Fred's memories of his following film were not pleasant: "*Eyes in the Night* was something of a nightmare. The plot involved a blind detective and his dog who somehow uncover a nest of Nazi spies. The problem was very simple. Man and dog had to be together in most scenes, but I had an actor who couldn't remember his lines and was only good on the eighth or ninth take, and a dog who was only good for one and who would then wander off and hide. We had to get a full-length feature out of this in five weeks. It's the kind of thing that could have made you an old man before your time because, of course, being a novice feature director, I was determined to do as good a job as possible. It seemed a terribly serious thing at the time.

Then the film came out and a caption to one of the reviews of it simply read: 'Dog bites Axis.' That reduced the situation to its proper importance and taught me a sense of proportion, which was a good lesson to learn in those days."

The film is more fun to watch than it clearly was to make. Edward Arnold hams entertainingly enough as the blind detective; Donna Reed is striking as the spoiled stepdaughter, anticipating her revelatory performance under Zinnemann's direction in *From Here to Eternity*; and the Nazis are played with some suaveness and intelligence , an early indication of the director's refusal to accept stereotyped characterization. A scene in a darkened apartment, where the blind man feels suddenly (as Milton would say) "in my kingdom," is atmospherically shot, and there is a torture scene which was to become something of a Zinnemann obsession. When the dog Friday takes over the plot and overwhelms the Nazis, the film's brain goes to sleep. A nice joke, where the dog, on his crucial mission, is not to be tempted by a flirtatious poodle, is a playful reference back to a similar gag in *Friend Indeed*.

"I then directed *The Seventh Cross*, which was undoubtedly the best of the films I did at that time. It was a wonderful story, by Anna Seghers, about seven prisoners escaping from a pre-war Nazi concentration camp. I found the basic situation fascinating. The man on the run for his life, played by Spencer Tracy, is a person who, simply by his presence, forces other people to get off the fence, on one side or another. No one can face him without taking a stand, and sometimes the stand that person takes surprises even himself. That one inarticulate workman, played by Hume Cronyn, who has thought that Hitler was a great man because everybody's working, finds in himself the courage to save his friend at the risk of his own and his family's lives. That was what I found strong and very affirmative in the story. The center of interest is not the hero but the vignettes of people's behavior in a situation where they *have* to take a position. I have always thought *The Seventh Cross* was a sort of cousin to *High Noon*. Structurally, the two films are very similar: basically, it's a man who is in need, who says help me, and the very cogent reasons most people find for not helping him."

The first part of the film is particularly preoccupied with

Heisler's escape from prison and the way his fear transforms every gaze into ambiguity or accusation and even infects the people he sees with his own apprehension and guilt. One person chases Heisler because he picks up the fugitive's sense of fear and mistakenly assumes that the man might have stolen his wallet. He has to apologize sheepishly to the police when he finds this is not so.

Because the film is so strikingly shot, with a memorable image of Heisler walking in fear and dread down a lonely road, and a fine scene evocative of *Frankenstein* (1931) when he tremulously encounters a child who might betray him, the atmosphere of prewar Germany is oppressively conveyed. The expressive sense of paranoia evokes Lang's *M* (1931), just as the casting of Tracy as the hunted man also summons up the specter of Lang's terrifying *Fury* (1936).

If the hero's terror infects his subjective viewpoint, his presence similarly tests the conscience of everyone he meets. He has had a demoralizing encounter with a former sweetheart (an idealized flashback scene exposing the fragility of the memory and anticipating the certainly of disillusionment) who is now married to an SS man. There are further edgy encounters with a costume designer (Agnes Moorehead) and a Jewish doctor, who may or may not recognize his situation and who may or may not be trying to help him. His main contact is arrested, the news relayed to him by a woman who opens her door to reveal a portrait of Hitler on the wall behind her: Heisler's nightmare writ large. (This part was played by Helene Veigel, the wife of Bertolt Brecht. There are various other distinguished German refugee-actors in the cast.) When he encounters one of the remaining fugitives, the latter tells him that he wishes to give himself up, an act which he knows is a symbolic suicide: It represents the correlative to Heisler's own hopelessness, his logical next step, the moment when he relinquishes his hold on life. In a final despairing gesture, he seeks help from an old friend, Paul (Hume Cronyn). Heisler hovers indecisively on the stairs, the kind of setting that Zinnemann was often to use for characters who are suddenly confused and unsure of their destination. The confession in *Act of Violence*, Philip's hesitant return home in *Teresa*, the shock revelation that Carlos is a traitor in *Behold a Pale Horse*, Lillian's awkward phone calls to

Spencer Tracy plays an escaped political prisoner on the run in pre-war Nazi Germany in *The Seventh Cross*, MGM, 1944.

an endangered Julia in *Julia* all take place on stairwells, a no-man's land between security and danger and in which a character's whole character and future might be influenced by the next step he takes. In *The Seventh Cross*, fate takes a hand. Heisler decides not to call but encounters Paul on the stairs and is pressured into staying for dinner. It is to be the saving of his life.

Unknown to Heisler and Paul, there is an Escape Committee working on his behalf who can help him but who cannot find him. Their job is bedevilled by their need for secrecy and by their ignorance of who they can trust, which is also the dilemma of Paul and Heisler. In a situation so fear-ridden and so redolent of betrayal, friends can look as menacing as enemies, and there is one moment where Heisler and Paul hide in terror from the very man who is trying to come to their rescue. The head of the Escape Committee discovers that Heisler has been staying at Paul's home, and knocks on the door. Terrified, Paul's wife (Jessica Tandy) only opens it as far as the chain will allow, the door dividing the screen down the middle in an extraordinary composition as a tense non-commital conversation takes place between two people who cannot see each other and cannot know that they are actually working for the same purpose.

There is a similar visual skill at work in another scene that is thematically rather like that one. Paul goes to see a former friend (George Macready) who is now a wealthy architect and who, initially, wants nothing to do with the fugitive. The house, with its elaborate décor and modern paintings, seems to extend Paul's psychological disorientation at his friend's situation and manner, a feeling climaxed by the moment when Paul's sense of moral and physical geography in this house is so confused that he cannot find his way out of the bathroom. The visual crystallization of this feeling consists of a brilliant split-screen mirror shot which makes it difficult for Paul (and the audience) to interpret the visual information assimilated by his own eyes. He suddenly feels himself to be in a hall of mirrors, a world that is distorted and grotesque.

Ultimately the rich friend agrees to help. Heisler is safely hidden in a hotel room, is helped by one of the hotel maids (Signe Hasso) and, for a night, loved and ultimately sails to freedom. His friend Paul is arrested on his way to work and Zinnemann, as he likes to do, conveys the drama of the moment and the character's confused state of mind in a single gesture: his incongruous, abstracted attempt to bundle his bicycle into the back of the police car. But later he is released.

One of the interesting things is the way in which Paul, almost unnoticed, becomes the film's main character. Heisler is frightened because he knows what awaits him, but he has already committed himself before and evinced a preparedness to suffer and maybe die for what he believes. The character of Paul is rather different and intrigues the director more, because he is impelled towards courage almost against his better judgment. He is apolitical, an ordinary family man, but a man who ultimately risks his life from a gut feeling that he could not continue to live with himself if, at this particular moment, he did not act in this one way. The courage of heroes is one thing; the courage of people who would prefer not to be heroes is quite another—and perhaps, in the long run, more noble.

"There is a word that I used to use: it's a German word, *zivilcourage*. It means, literally, 'civilian courage,' and the courage of an individual in standing up to an institution or standing out against public opinion because of the dictates of his own conscience. There is in many of my films this crucial moment when people realize what they must do: either consciously, in a very articulate way, like Sir Thomas More in *A Man for All Seasons*, or instinctively, like the Marshal in *High Noon*."

When asked why he stayed in Germany during the Nazi period, the great conductor Wilhelm Furtwängler (one of Zinnemann's heroes) replied: "It would have been much easier to emigrate, but there had to be a spiritual center of integrity for all the good and real Germans who had to stay behind. I felt that a really great work of music was a stronger and more essential contradiction to the spirit of Buchenwald and Auschwitz than words could be." Furtwängler's difficult relationship with the Nazis (recalling the actor's outburst in Szabo's 1981 film *Mephisto*: "A whole country cannot emigrate!") must have been full of the agonizing moral choices so characteristic of the Zinnemann hero. And his phrase about the "good and real Germans" is absolutely central to the feeling of *The Seventh Cross* and its refusal to whip up nationalist hatred from glib generalization. Not every German was a Nazi and a monster between 1933 and 1945. *The Seventh Cross* is one of the few Hollywood films of the period which attempts to counter the Nazi stereotype.

Zinnemann told me, "*The Seventh Cross* is one of my films that I sometimes think I'd like to do again. In those days I did not have a say on the script. The narration, full of sentimental rubbish, is something I would gladly have done without. The studio sets and back-projection look false to me now. Nowadays I would like to do it in real surroundings with German people and actors. Then that was not possible. It was a great experience, though, working with actors of the caliber of Spencer Tracy, Hume Cronyn and Jessica Tandy. I found Tracy enormously impressive. His reputation was formidable even then. At that time MGM had a lot of young actors under contract, and when the word was out that Tracy was doing a scene, all these young people were clustered around watching—Gene Kelly, Van Johnson, Bob Walker—seeing what they could learn. Tracy did very little that was visible to the naked eye. You could be standing ten feet away from him and he would be doing hardly anything, and yet when you saw it up on the screen, the power of the man just seemed to explode."

After the exhilarating experience of *The Seventh Cross* in 1943, a period of disillusionment followed. He was assigned to direct the film *The Clock*, but was removed after a fortnight's shooting, apparently because the star, Judy Garland, felt she was not getting enough help from Zinnemann. Talking to me of the experience later, Zinnemann believed that Judy acted in a professional and honorable way, and rejected the idea that, as she was in love with Vincente Minnelli and Minnelli was assigned to take over, the whole thing had been planned before the film started shooting. "I think it was just that Judy was insecure and I, as a journeyman director, didn't know how to help her. I thought she was doing very well, but she didn't. It happens sometimes. A lot of location material had been shot in the Metropolitan Museum in New York and around Fifth Avenue, but none of it was incorporated into the final film."

Now the studio decided to put him back into the B-picture division. Bound by a cast-iron contract which stipulated that the director was obligated to carry out all instructions of the Front Office, Zinnemann could not refuse. He was clearly at a crucial point in his career. "It was now that my reputation as a rebel and a troublemaker came about. I had no such reputation in the Shorts Department: I cannot remember protesting about anything there. But now I started turning down scripts. The Front Office sent me a script which I thought was awful and I said, 'Sorry, I don't want to do it.' To my surprise they said 'Okay.' Then they sent me another, and I said, 'This is even worse than the last one, sorry.' I was getting paid all this time. Eyebrows were raised. So when I said 'No' to the third script they sent for me..."

Suspension and Success

"I was called to the office of MGM's general manager, who was a very tough Irishman called Eddie Mannix. He'd started life as a bouncer for Joe Schenck and was a very straight shooter. 'Look,' he said to me, 'you're paid to do what the boss tells you and if you do that, we take care of you. You could be a very valuable property for the studio, but you've got to obey orders. The best directors I have—' he mentioned two who were actually the worst, 'just do as they're told.' Then he looked me straight in the eye and said: 'You're perfectly aware that MGM never makes a bad picture.' My face never twitched. He went on: 'If there's something wrong with it, after the preview we'll fix it, so I want you just to go ahead and make this picture.' 'I don't know what to do with it,' I said. 'In that case,' he said heavily, 'I'll have to suspend you.' Being naïve, I thought for a moment and said, 'What does that mean?' He looked surprised, but explained: 'It means that, as of today, you will go off salary and will not be paid anything until after the film you've turned down has been shot, edited and delivered to the theaters.' I knew that would take about six months. He went on: 'Also, of course, you can't work anywhere else because you're under contract here.' I thought this over for a moment and then said: 'Okay, I'll go on suspension.'

"Mannix looked amazed, but called in the Company lawyer to do the legal papers. The lawyer was a terribly nice man called Floyd Hendrickson and he looked taken aback. The studio had a bush telegraph, everyone knew everything almost before it happened. My meeting with Mannix had been private but when I went back on the lot, I seemed to be surrounded by people who knew what had happened. They started clapping me on the back, as though I had got the Purple Heart or something. Three or four weeks later, Mannix called me back and said: 'Look, I've been trying to find a reason to put you back on the payroll and I can't find one. So I'll put you back anyway. After all, no one objects when Victor Fleming and Clarence Brown turn down scripts.' He was a fair fighter, Mannix was.

"I then made *Little Mister Jim* [1946] and *My Brother Talks to Horses* [1947], about which the less said the better. Curiously enough, that aura of being a non-conformist stuck for quite a while. Producers, especially B-picture producers, avoided me like the plague. The Administration building was known to MGM employees as either the 'White Elephant' or the 'Iron Lung.' It was a long, long building and as you came in at one end there was a corridor stretching seemingly into infinity. At this time I would come in and see a producer coming round the corner, a tiny figure. As soon as he spotted me, I could see him stop and think how to escape. He would either turn back and go into his office, or he'd take a side door that led to the toilet or go upstairs.

"I wasn't exactly a pariah, for there were many people who tried to be helpful, according to their own lights. The casting director, Billy Grady, said to me once: 'Look, you're too persnickety. Why don't you just go ahead and cooperate? People are going to start thinking of you as a troublemaker.' Finally, salvation appeared in the form of Lazar Wechsler, a Swiss producer, and of Arthur Loew, president of MGM's overseas distribution. It was now mid-1946. Wechsler and Loew approached MGM with an idea to do a picture in Switzerland about displaced children, orphans of the Second World War. This is to be known later as *The Search*. It was going to be financed by Loews International. Wechsler asked if he could borrow me to direct the film. The reaction was, I understand, 'By all means.' I was asked if I would like to do it and, of course, I jumped at it. So I disappeared for a year. Then the picture was finished and we brought it back to run it for the upper echelon of MGM. The projection room was at the end of the 'White Elephant' in the cellar. The bush telegraph must have been working again because after an hour people seemed to be hearing that it was a good movie. I came out and stood in the same spot as the one I had stood in before. This time all doors were opening, people were coming into big close-ups rather than disappearing in a long shot. They were patting me on the back and saying, 'We knew you had it in you, kid.' It was hilarious, but I think it made a cynic out of me."

There is a postscript to this story. It offers an insight into the way the studio system worked. The director who eventually did the film Zinnemann turned down brought it in three days under schedule and under budget. The grateful studio gave him a bonus of several thousand dollars. The studio then previewed the film. The next day, the director was fired.

CHAPTER TWO

The Aftermath of War

The Search *(1948)*

Producer Lazar Wechsler had the idea for *The Search* from a fine book of photographs by Therese Bonney called *Europe's Children*. He had thought of Fred Zinnemann as director after seeing *The Seventh Cross*. At the outset, Wechsler, Zinnemann and the writer, Richard Schweizer, agreed that they ought to get as many of the elements of the story as possible from first-hand observation, visiting the actual camps in occupied Germany and talking to as many displaced persons as possible. Wechsler and Bonney obtained permission from the military to visit all the UNRRA camps (the United Nations Relief and Rehabilitation Agency). "We would talk to the camp commander first and then to selected people. We heard many of the stories that have much later become familiar through the Eichmann trial and through thousands of books, except that we were hearing them from the victims themselves and shortly after the War, when these horrors were still fresh in their minds. So the research was all the more harrowing."

The difficulty was that, after researching the material and

being overwhelmed by the enormity of what they had seen, Wechsler and Zinnemann still did not have a storyline, only hundreds of case histories. Richard Schweizer had not accompanied them on the research because he had pneumonia. When he was told of the problem, he said: "Why not make the film around a mother trying to find her young son who was separated from her during the War?" It was an inspiration and suddenly everything fell into place.

Parts of the film were shot on location in the bombed-out ruins of Munich, Nuremberg and Frankfurt and the interiors were shot under primitive conditions in Zurich, with a small crew, not a lot of money and not much film to play with because at that time in Switzerland it was scarce and expensive. Most of the children in the film had actually come from concentration camps. Permission was obtained from the United Nations to approach them and explain the purpose of the film, at the same time warning them that the experience might revive memories that were extremely painful. If they wished to volunteer, that was fine; there was no pressure on them to do so. All of them volunteered.

The children were content until it was time to shave their heads and dress them in their concentration camp clothes, at which point they understandably became tense and distressed. The boy who played the main part, Ivan Jandl, was a Czech and knew German. But when Zinnemann tried to talk to him in German, the boy would not react, and Zinnemann finally had to direct him through a Czech interpreter. German reminded him of the Nazi occupation and produced a mental block that must have been similar to that described by Sylvia Plath in her semi-autobiographical novel *The Bell Jar*, when recalling traumatic memories of her German-speaking parents: "Each time I picked up a German dictionary or German book, the very sight of those dense, black, barbed-wire letters made my mind shut like a clam."

It was easy to see what such authenticity of feeling could bring to the film, but at the same time it was disturbing. Zinnemann remembered particularly a scene in the UNRRA office where the supervisor (Aline MacMahon) enters the room and the children have to show fear at the sight of her uniform: "We didn't have enough children for this scene, so we added a group of Swiss children, and I explained the scene to them, and asked them to react as I had indicated. But nothing happened, they just looked blank. They did not know the meaning of fear. When I asked the children who had been in the camps to do the scene, the difference was amazing, harrowing. They knew the terror that can be conveyed by a uniform from their own experience."

The casting worked out particularly successfully. Aline MacMahon was an experienced film and theater actress who brought enormous authority to her role, whilst Jarmila Novotna, who played the mother, had been a great opera star who scaled down her performance very effectively for the film.

The revelation was Montgomery Clift as the American soldier. Clift had been recommended to Zinnemann by a good friend, Peter Viertel, who had been extremely impressed by him on stage. He had already made one film, *Red River*, for Howard Hawks, but that film had not yet been released. (In the event, *The Search* came out before the Hawks film.) The two men met and discussed the project (at that time there was still no script) and, on the basis of that meeting, they decided to take a chance on each other. Impressed by Clift's personality and his enthusiasm for the material, Zinnemann trusted to instinct. Such instincts were to serve him and others very well through the years. Clift, Marlon Brando (in *The Men*), Rod Steiger (*Teresa*), Julie Harris (*The Member of the Wedding*), John Hurt (*A Man for All Seasons*) and Meryl Streep (*Julia*) are only a few of the brilliant performers who were to make their first big screen impression in a Zinnemann film.

"I was convinced Monty Clift would be fine because he was a charming, vital, electrifying personality who seemed prepared to take a chance on the film and on me. The idea of travelling to Europe appealed to him because at that time nobody was going to Europe, which was still in ruins, and because then it was something of an adventure to be shooting a film on location. Whether it was China in *The Good Earth* or whatever, previously it was all recreated inside a studio stage or the back lot."

The Search is a film in which one can feel realism coursing through it like a tonic serum. It is a film fired by the example of Italian neo-realism, if not overtly influenced by it (in its location shooting, its use of little-known actors rather than stars to intensify audience identification, its post-war setting, the urgency and seriousness of its theme and its stress on the experience of children). It is also a film which draws strength from a post-war situation in Hollywood in which both audiences and filmmakers seemed more prepared to face realism on the screen and less susceptible to the usual escapism. Films such as *The Lost Weekend* (1945), *The Best Years of Our Lives* (1946), *Gentleman's Agreement* (1947), *Home of the Brave* (1947), *Crossfire* (1947) and *Body and Soul* (1947) showed a new willingness of Hollywood to deal in dramatic terms with controversial themes. Directors like William Wyler, John Ford, John Huston, Frank Capra and George Stevens had served in the war as filmmakers. They returned affected by their experiences, a change which was reflected in their immediate post-war work. *The Search* has a slightly different inflection. It seems characteristic of the kind of film made by a director still at heart a European. It talks honestly not only about the horror of the European experience, but of the American response to that experience.

A good example of this is the scene when the American family of Stevenson's friend, Jerry Fisher (Wendell Corey), arrive at Fisher's flat. The American boy boasts of his family's standard of living; the European boy is painfully rediscovering the quality of life. Around the dinner table, the wife is rather surprised that the boy looks quite well and can speak English and she behaves towards him as a foreigner to be talked about rather than to be addressed in person. This awkwardness is emphasized in the scene's visual organization, with the child under discussion actually being excluded from the frame for much of the time. Suddenly the American boy has soup accidentally spilled on him and he runs simpering into the arms of his mother. One cannot help comparing the American boy's reaction to a scalded hand and the refugee's tight-lipped stoicism about his horrific experience. Indeed, it has been his *refusal* to cry out in pain earlier—when the soldiers have put iodine on his injured foot—that has caused them to wonder who he is and about his former existence. The shot of American mother and son is not an image of ideal family life endorsed by the film and to which the refugee aspires. It seems rather the shot of a pampered child and matriarch, watched by a boy whose own pain these people can scarcely begin to comprehend. It raises the whole question of the role and attitude of Americans in the film.

Two—The Aftermath of War

The American soldier who helps the boy is well-meaning and kindly but does not know how to deal with a wild, panicky child. It is to Montgomery Clift's great credit (and one of the reasons why the performance is such a remarkable one) that he understands this so well, refusing to turn the man into an American boy scout and instead offering a portrayal of a sensitive and caring man impulsively trying to come to terms with a situation which he is at first ill-equipped to handle. The American's actions are sometimes clumsy—at one stage he even threatens the boy with a hypodermic needle—but his instincts are generous and positive.

The relationship between the two is sensitively done. The American first sees him in the rubble of Munich and tempts him with food, like an animal. It is a reminder of the boy's previous bestial existence, and of the arrival of the children at the UNRRA camp in cattle trucks, their pale faces illuminated by the single light of Mrs. Murray's flashlight (a very characteristic Zinnemann shot of the pervading darkness precariously pierced by a single source of light). The animal imagery is extended as the boy follows the American like a faithful dog and has the concept of mother explained to him through animal pictures. Such imagery reaches its climax when the boy knocks over Fisher's goldfish bowl, a moment which characterizes both the boy's and the Americans' state as that of "fish out of water." The goldfishes' gasping for breath recalls the boy's near drowning and his death-in-life at the prison camp. Their rescue by the Americans anticipates his fate.

Stevenson initiates a program in which the lad is to learn English and prides himself in his skill, though the hint is given that the boy had learned English at home (the mother speaks good English) and is remembering the language rather than being taught from scratch. This education is offered mainly in the form of pictures of New York, of Abraham Lincoln, even of Bambi. It is as if he is educating the boy into the ways of America, and his gift to him at the UNRRA camp is to be that most American of symbols, a baseball bat. Yet the visual strategy of the film is precisely to reverse that. If education is a key theme in *The Search*, it is not the education of the European to the ways of America but the education of the American audience to what happened in Europe. Like Stevenson, Zinnemann does it by pictures.

He does it by evoking a family background for the boy that is strikingly different in kind from the life of the American family. The boy's father is a doctor and amateur musician (interestingly, like Zinnemann's own father), and family life there is presented in the form of chamber music, with father, mother and daughter playing a trio, and the son writing at a desk. The image is both intensely European (it is one of Zinnemann's own memories of his early life in Vienna) and an image of a cultural background which the Nazis are brutally to destroy. This destruction is signalled here by a jarring ring of the doorbell which cuts atonally across the music's harmony, and by a fade from a shot of some branches visible through a window of their home to a shot of the window of their camp with barbed wire outside.

Similar window shots are to recur in the film, indicative of spurned people trying to re-enter, involve themselves again in the world: like the mother at the chapel, looking through the window for her son whose discovery at that point would alone give her life meaning; like the son later, who has run away from the dinner party into town and looks through the window of a house in search of his mother. Their parting at the prison camp has been shot from behind the wire, the mist across the screen giving the scene a ghostly, nightmarish aura. Such imagery is to gather cumulative resonances. The boy flinches at the sight of the railings outside the Americans' house because they remind him of prison bars; bridge railings are reflected in the river like bars when the mother thinks of suicide after being told her son is dead; the boy suddenly starts drawing lines across paper as a signal that he is remembering his parting from his mother. Faded Nazi insignia on the UNRRA walls chillingly evoke the hateful memories that can never be entirely erased from the children's minds. Such pictures of a devastated Europe and suffering children are really directed at an American audience in the hope of opening their eyes to a horror they could not possibly have grasped.

Even Stevenson never grasps why the boy seems to have a mental block over the word "umbrella" (it is that "umbrella" subconsciously summons up the memory of his mother). But one gesture reveals the kind of sensitivity which might enable him to help the boy. When he has demonstrated to the boy that he is free to go, the boy runs out into the street. It is a familiar Zinnemann situation of a person's feeling himself pursued, even when no one is following, because it represents that character's own sense of inner fear. (There is to be a superb example of that in *Act of Violence*, and also at the beginning of *Teresa*.) But the boy stops and then turns back. "It is not a conscious decision, it is purely instinct. His turning around expresses the inner change in him, just as, when Gary Cooper turns his buggy round to go back to the town in *High Noon*, the gesture is a physical expression of a change of mind. At this point the child has decided that perhaps it *is* possible to trust someone, that there is still some hope in the world. It's the moment when he gives up being hunted like an animal, when he starts to believe that perhaps he is not all alone."

The film, then, is poised between offering an American view of Europe and a European view of Americans. This kind of duality is elaborated in the film both structurally and stylistically. Structurally, it is suggested through the two plots—mother seeking son, son seeking mother—which run parallel but do not converge until the last moment when mother and child cross in a visual design that seems to echo the movement of the narrative. It is a narrative design which Zinnemann seemed to favor—there are elements of it in *The Seventh Cross, Act of Violence, From Here to Eternity, Behold a Pale Horse, Day of the Jackal*—and it recalls the reference in the narration to those countries once dominated by the Third Reich with their "broad, parallel, endless roads," a moment accompanied by superb imagery which seems visually to suggest the dual plot structure.

Stylistically, *The Search* walks a tightrope between two seemingly contradictory impulses. It is a film of documentary authenticity yet also one of some narrative contrivance and sentimentality (the preparation for the reunion of mother and son towards the end is extended in a rather confected way and there is a patronizing narration which was added to the film behind Zinnemann's back). The film is emotional drama, stiffened with neo-realist steel, building a bridge across two distinct styles in order to make a mass audience film that entertains without falsifying truth or reality.

"Let's reconstruct a kid's life for a change, instead of bridges," says Stevenson, who has previously been building a model bridge in the apartment. It is a theme taken up by *Act of Violence*, where post-war reconstruction is seen not simply in terms of places but also of people. *The Search* sees this in terms of reunion: *Act of Violence* is to see it in terms of confrontation. The Old World might give way to the New, but *The Search* is interesting for what it has to say about Europe and America—particularly of an America full of good will, yet not in a position to understand a kind of suffering that is totally outside of its own experience.

Act of Violence *(1949)*

After an explosive outburst of Bronislau Kaper music and an unmistakable establishing shot of a rainy New York, a man limps out of the shadows and painfully climbs the stairs to his small room. He slams a newspaper onto a table and takes a gun from the drawer, facing the camera for the first time as he loads it. He boards a coach for Los Angeles, alighting at Santa Lisa, and books a room in his name "Joe Parkson." Looking through the phone book, he circles the name "Frank Enley." There is an immediate cut to Enley (Van Heflin) with his son on his shoulders and his wife Edith (Janet Leigh) at his side, proud that her husband is being feted for his vital part in sustaining a community building program. "On the double, Captain," says the announcer, as he invites Enley to take a bow, adding that Frank "helped keep our spirits up ... the flesh was willing but the spirit was pretty low...."

This opening exposition of character and situation is masterly. The introduction to Parkson (Robert Ryan) is classic film noir. Out of a background of shadow, rain and the city, a hate-filled character emerges whose disability, as with characters in films such as *Double Indemnity* (1944) and *The Big Heat* (1953), is felt symbolically and psychologically as well as physically. The film reveals later that Parkson's newspaper has contained Enley's picture and it is this that has revived Parkson's hate and precipitated his journey. Ironically, then, this celebration for Enley and his family has also dragged Parkson into the picture, a dark shadow across the festivities and this all–American family. When Parkson arrives in Santa Lisa, the coach pulls up across the townspeople's remembrance

Two—The Aftermath of War 39

of the "Solemn Rites of Memorial Day" and Parkson walks across the road between that point in the parade which separates soldiers and civilians, momentarily disrupting its smooth continuity. It represents the limbo between wartime and civilian life in which Parkson now moves. It is also an anticipation of the way in which Parkson's revelations about the war are to sever Enley's own continuity from war to ordinary life.

During the coach ride to Santa Lisa, Parkson has never once looked out of the window: He has his eyes set on where he is going. His obsession is also suggested by the distance he has to travel to exact his revenge (crossing the continent from New York to California). Interestingly, however, the journey is from night to day. This begins to complicate the light/dark symbolism and to suggest that an initial assumption of Parkson as villain and Enley as hero needs immediate qualification. As the film develops, it becomes clear that Parkson represents not evil as such but the dark side of Enley which must be brought to light. He is the chill across Enley's "noontide of prosperity" (to quote Charles Lamb), the fearful fiend of guilt that Enley dare not confront. He is Enley's shadow, invariably appearing *behind* him. Parkson's scenes with Enley's wife take place during the day as part of the dramatic scheme whereby he must expose the man she has married. Correspondingly, Enley becomes increasingly a figure of the night, as he tries to hide from this self-revelation. A startling shot which picks up these motifs has Enley at an L.A. Builders' Convention turning to see Parkson behind him in a light raincoat, visually removed from the seething humanity below and resembling an Avenging Angel relentlessly in search of his wretched quarry.

In retrospect, then, the introduction to Enley is highly ironic. He is introduced as a typical family man with a young wife (a symbol of his attempt at a fresh start?) and with a job in construction (an attempt to rebuild his life?). Significantly, but also ominously, he is addressed as "Captain," which is a reminder of the war. Significantly, but also ominously, his son is on his shoulders. The son is to be a burden throughout the film, another emblem of guilt that Enley has to carry around. (How will his son react in the future if Enley's name is dragged through the papers by Parkson? His son is the reason Enley cannot go to the police.) Like his father, the child seems to be plagued by nightmares, twice roused by the presence of Parkson near the house, and twice used as a shock effect, his screams an external expression of his infection by his father's fear. (Another emblem of the guilt Enley is carrying on his shoulders is his old Army jacket, which Edith tries to make him take on his fishing trip and which he pointedly throws out of the car.) Towards the end of the film, when Enley looks in on his sleeping son, all we see are the bars of the cot, an image which links with Enley's prison camp experience and ties in the child as being all part of Enley's sense of himself as a trapped man.

Prior to Enley's awareness that Parkson is following him, there is a brief scene at home when he is searching for his rod for his fishing trip. It is the last comfortable domestic scene in the film, indeed the last scene of any kind of repose. His search for his rod in the shadowy corner seems to anticipate the "skeletons in the cupboard" theme that is to erupt later. Enley's buoyant confidence with his wife at this stage will contrast painfully with their final scene together. "I'm getting used to you ... you've lost you glamour," says Edith to him, playfully, ironically, in this early scene. In their final conversation, Edith has to say the same thing, gravely, understandingly, painfully ("Up until yesterday, I thought you were the finest, most wonderful man in the world ... I now see you have your faults and weaknesses, like any man. But it doesn't mean I don't still love you"). The domestic banter also draws attention to the importance of homes in the film. Characters are very aware of their settings, each representing an aspect of the character's psychology (e.g. Enley's respectable façade, Parkson's bitter gloom). The emphasis on place gives particular weight to the moment when Enley, late in the film, tells the prostitute that he has "no place to go." When self-respect is lost, there is no home.

There are three subsequent substantial episodes between Enley and his wife in the film. Two take place at their homes: the dramatic entrance of Parkson into their domestic life early on; and a later scene when they try to reconstruct what that entrance has destroyed. In between comes Enley's crucial confession, appropriately rendered away from the home, just as the revelation itself threatens the domestic arrangement Enley has painstakingly constructed. The first of these scenes occurs when Enley has become

The domestic tranquility of the Enley household is about to be disrupted by the revelation of a dark secret from Enley's wartime past. Janet Leigh as Edith Enley (left) and Van Heflin as Frank Enley (right) in M-G-M's *Act of Violence*, 1949.

aware that Parkson is hunting him, and he abruptly terminates his fishing holiday and returns home. The domestic dialogue is counter pointed and contradicted by the imagery, as Enley nervously forbids Edith to answer the phone (every phone call from now on in the film is to be significant and menacing) and pulls down the blinds. It intensifies a sense of claustrophobia, their home as a prison. It also emphasizes Enley's forlorn attempt to establish his home as a hiding place, shutting out the reality, the past outside. When the doorbell rings, the coffee percolator hisses unattended and the camera prowls over to the back door as Parkson limps round to test the entrance. It is an aural rendering of the hate Parkson is dragging around with him. It is also the sound of Enley's guilt, the albatross that will always pull him back from security, prosperity, happiness.

In fact, the final scene between Enley and his wife at their home shows that this domestic dream has gone forever. When Enley returns, he is framed in the doorway exactly as Parkson has been earlier when he has visited: now a stranger to the former contentment. The scene that follows between him and his wife is a brilliantly conceived and executed parody of domestic bliss. Child upstairs sleeping, wife downstairs sewing, husband reading the paper—what could be more emblematic of contented family life? But we only see the *bars* of the cot and not the child itself; the wife is sewing because she can hardly bear to look at her husband; she has handed him the paper almost as a way of preventing him from coming nearer, from touching her. Every item of domestic bliss is undermined. "Edith, I think I heard the baby cry," he says, and as she goes up the stairs to check, he sneaks out of the house and the nightmare resumes.

The reason for the deterioration of the relationship is provided in Enley's confession. During the war, in return for promises of food, Enley has given away the details of an escape plan to the German prison guards and, in the process, all but Parkson have been brutally murdered. The confession is expressively staged on a darkened, deserted stairway with only a single lamp to illuminate the scene. Such a staging not only infuses ominous shadows into the images but it puts Enley under an oppressive spotlight. It is one of Zinnemann's characteristic interrogation scenes that become a form of self-interrogation. At one moment Enley clings to the railings of the staircase like a prisoner at the bar, and his dreadful self-revelation in this bleak setting powerfully evokes Fritz Lang's *M*. Later when Enley runs from Parkson out of the Convention, the pursuer is not seen, and it is as if Enley is being chased by himself, by the Furies. It is exactly the feeling incomparably conveyed in Peter Lorre's monologue in *M* as he tries to explain his evil impulses: "I want to run away. I have to run away. I am always forced to move along streets, and someone is always behind me. It is I, I am myself behind me, and yet I cannot escape."

During his flight from Parkson, Enley runs under a bridge at the precise time when two trolley cars cross but do not meet. It is an evocative image of the two characters, and a strong motif in other Zinnemann films (previously *The Seventh Cross* and *The*

Search and subsequently, *Behold a Pale Horse* and *Julia*) where the narratives and destinies of two people are strongly linked but tantalizingly separate. It is at this point that Enley runs into the prostitute (brilliantly played by Mary Astor). From here the second movement of the film begins, a movement particularly dominated by money.

There are only two kinds of trouble, believes the prostitute: love trouble or money trouble. "With money you can fix everything," she declares. In fact, in a film of Zinnemann's, the troubles are rarely to do with love or money, and Enley's gesture of rubbing his head furiously (as if physically trying to drive out the torments inside him) locates where the trouble usually emanates: from inside the individual's head. Indeed, the failed attempt to buy off Parkson carries quite large resonances in the film. It signifies the limitations of money as a real solution to the problems of an America, many of whose men are still traumatized by the war .

Enley descends further into the "night world" and the proposition of hiring a killer is put to him. It is a world with its own law, outside the boundaries of justice; oddly, its morality parallels Parkson's own scheme of revenge ("Are you the judge of that, are you the Law?" Anne has asked Parkson about his vendetta against Enley). As Enley tells all to a shady lawyer in an oppressively bleak setting, the camera roams over to the door and a bar-shaped shadow forms under the crack. It is the figure of the hired killer, Johnny, who is listening outside. Johnny is a kind of Devil, a tempter, a man with no address, who seems to be serving Enley's interests but, as the camera movement implies, is actually menacing him as Parkson is. (Indeed, he is to do to Enley what the latter fears from Parkson—kill him.)

"He dies, or you die, it's him or you," says the lawyer to Enley. "You're the same man you were in Germany. You did it once, you'll do it again." This is perhaps the bluntest statement of the "Character as Destiny" theme in Zinnemann's early work, which is to become so important in his future films. Enley flees into the subway and the voices in his head are unnaturally heightened by the tunnel, recalling the escape tunnel of his murdered comrades (a similar image is to occur in a nightmarish context in *Julia*) and with his flight checked by barbed wire which recalls the prison camp. He contemplates suicide but has not the courage to stand in front of the oncoming train. The deal is made with Johnny in a booze-soaked oblivion: A meeting is arranged with Parkson.

The final scene is beautifully laid out, the coming of night signifying the recurrence of Enley's nightmare. Uncomprehendingly Enley passes Parkson's fiancée, another example of two characters who are linked yet separate, with parallel obsessions. He all but ignores a newspaper boy who calls him by name, for Enley is now no longer interested in his "picture in the paper," the picture that has brought the trouble down on him. The sound of the train recalls Enley's contemplated suicide, and oddly anticipates *High Noon* in which a character similarly recognizes that he must "face a man who hates him." But again, the anticipated confrontation (like the moment on the lake when Parkson has been squaring up to shoot Enley) suddenly goes off at a crazy angle. Spotting Johnny lining up Parkson in his sights, Enley comes between them, caught in a crossfire between the desire to expunge and the desire to atone. Reeling from the gunshot wounds, he clings to Johnny's escaping car, the imagery suddenly matching Enley's life and fate: a man being tossed crazily about by a chaotic force before being thrown free. The police arrive belatedly, but the dialogue is as bare and bleak as anything in Lang or Siodmak. "Call Emergency Hospital," says the cop and then, taking a closer look at Enley adds, "Never mind." "Who's going to tell his wife?" asks someone in the crowd. Parkson looks up and says, "I will." There is an odd ambiguity about this end. What has Parkson left to live for, now that Enley is dead? In walking away, it is noticeable that he does *not* take his fiancée by the arm: There is no sense of fresh beginnings, but a man returning to the night.

As a film noir, *Act of Violence* has considerable potency both visually and thematically. It relates the picture of a troubled America to the consequences of the war. In other films of this kind, the genre's Expressionist imagery has often been related to the director's angst-ridden European background and the genre's misogyny has been related to a masculine fear of a new-found feminine independence that has flourished in his absence. In *Act of Violence*, this is inflected somewhat differently. Enley and Parkson are the archetypal tormented heroes of film noir, but their resentment of the women derives from their sense that the women missed the torment they went through. "A lot of things happened in the war that you don't understand," Enley says to Edith. His attitude recalls the prostitute: that love and money trouble are the only kind that women understand, and the fundamental problems—trauma, pride, self-respect, cowardice, physical danger—are basically masculine concerns. "You don't know what made him the way he is," says Enley to his wife, "I do" (only too true, but the rebuke should be directed against himself, not her). Parkson's fiancée, Anne, says that "they're both sick with it," i.e., the war, but the women also suffer because of this sickness. What the film is defining in these relationships is an extremely dark analogue of the relation of men and women to war itself: men being thrust into a situation with which they psychologically cannot cope; women having to watch their men become murderers.

Typically, for Zinnemann, the concept of war is internalized more than externalized: His characters invariably have rival warring factions at loose inside their heads. The film's centerpiece is Enley's confession and his revelation of himself as an informer against his colleagues to save his own skin. In that scene, the film suddenly becomes not about a war in the past that took place in Europe, but about a Cold War in the present that is taking part in the heart of America. Its uncompromising emphasis on Enley as "informer" and its refusal to countenance his behavior as anything other than cowardice must have struck some uncomfortable chords in the Hollywood of 1949, a community fearfully under the scrutiny of the House of Un-American Activities Committee and where dubious, pragmatic alliances were being formed from motives that had less to do with patriotism than self-interest. "You can always find reasons—even the Nazis had reasons," says Enley. In its allusions to cowardice, confession and community, *Act of Violence* is a dark, eloquent commentary on the times.

The Men *(1950)*

After *Act of Violence* and the conclusion of his seven-year contract with MGM, Zinnemann was glad to get away from the work routine of a major studio. His agent, the legendary Abe Lastfogel, strongly advised him not to accept any script he did not like, even if it should take months. Script submissions from other studios soon dwindled to nothing, but during all this time Lastfogel supported him, finally even financially. It was a year before rescue arrived.

It came in the form of a very fine screenplay by Carl Foreman, *The Men*. It seemed an ideal project. If *The Search* and *Act of Violence* had concentrated on the psychological aftermath of war, *The Men* was concerned with the physical: the rehabilitation of paraplegics. In fact, in looking at the problems experienced by one particular paraplegic, Ken Wilozek (Marlon Brando), who is alienated from his fellow patients and his fiancée Ellen (Teresa Wright), the film sees the rehabilitation as a matter of mind as well as body.

The producer of the film was Stanley Kramer, who after the war had established a reputation (with such films as *Home of the Brave* and *Champion*) as the brightest and most adventurous of the new independent producers. Kramer had first become aware of Zinnemann in the Shorts Department at MGM, where Kramer himself had worked as an editor and as a short-lived assistant to Pete Smith. "There were various things that convinced me Fred would be a good addition to the team," Kramer told me. "We were a small company with a modest budget and at that time Fred did not come too expensively. I had liked *The Search* very much and felt that he was a very 'pure' director—he can get big emotional effects in the simplest way by going for the truth of the scene; there was nothing fancy about him. And, in addition to talent, I felt his personality was what we wanted. He had his own ideas but he would work as part of a team."

The first decision concerned the approach the film would follow in order to lend conviction and authenticity to the subject. Kramer, Zinnemann and Foreman all agreed that, even if desirable, it would be impossible to film in an actual hospital and disturb the routine of nurses and patients. The reality should come from people, not from the walls of their surroundings, using paraplegic patients of a Veterans' Hospital in some of the roles together with the remainder of the cast. The effectiveness of integrating actors and non-actors had already been demonstrated in Italy in such neo-realist masterpieces as Rossellini's *Rome—Open City* (1945). In Hollywood, Wyler had had an enormous success in directing a real-life amputee, Harold Russell, in the fictional *The Best Years of Our Lives*. *The Men* seems to owe much to *Best Years* in its casting of Teresa Wright in the sympathetic woman's role and Ray Teal as a patronizing civilian, and in its similar perceptions about traumatized men and strong women in a troubled New World.

If Zinnemann had suggested using actual paraplegics at MGM, there would have been an argument, but Kramer was excited by the idea. It was a bracing experience to be able to exchange views and deal so directly with the people who had ultimate responsibility for the picture. The casting began. "We interviewed about 50 volunteers and out of those we picked about 14. It was interesting because the paraplegics were all in there for different reasons. Some were in there for tragic reasons, others not so heroic. One was there because he'd been shot in the back by the husband of the girl he was in bed with; another had fallen off a motorcycle, and so on."

Because they were playing opposite real patients, the main actors needed to have that extra edge of truth in their performances. It was agreed that the actors in the main roles should be relatively unknown, without the resonances of a "star" persona. This was a factor, though not the only one, in the decision to cast Marlon Brando, who had not made a film before. Kramer had seen him on stage as Stanley Kowalski in *A Streetcar Named Desire* and thought he would be a fine actor for the main role. Kramer confessed that as the tempestuous Brando and the reserved Zinnemann were completely different personalities, he had some anxiety about their possible working relationship. To his delight, they got on famously, mutually trusting each other's instincts and respecting the sincerity with which each, in his own way, wanted what was best for the film. In preparing himself for the part, Brando lived on the ward with the patients for over three weeks. He learned to think and react as they did, sharing the feelings of men who face not only horrendous pain but the certainty that their condition is incurable and the prospect of total change in the pattern of their previous lives.

The film is very clear-sighted about two particular aspects of the paraplegics' dilemma: sex and economics. When one disabled veteran marries a nurse, the cynic of the ward, Norm (Jack Webb), is quick to observe that the nurse will receive more money as the wife of a disabled veteran than from being a nurse on the ward. The attribution of mercenary motives for marriage in this context is not really a reflection on the nurse, for there is no way of knowing whether this observation is justified or not. But it does afford a revealing insight into the anxieties of the men themselves, the way in which their condition transforms their vision of women into one of protective cynicism or nightmarish apprehension. The film is quite frank about the likely impotence of the men, Dr. Brock (Everett Sloane) offering little hope to one of the wives who in an early scene asks: "Can we have a family?" (Dr. Brock was based on a real character, Dr. Ernest Bors, whom Zinnemann described to me as "a magnificent man who saved countless lives.") The film's honesty about this leads to one of its most interesting developments: the redefinition of the masculine role in a situation where he has to be dependent on the female.

This theme is superbly expressed through the developing understanding between Ken and Ellen. Their relationship after Ken's injury is initially full of tension, partly because of his fear of her pity, and partly because of her illusions that the condition might be reversible. Their awkward first meeting in the film takes place against the background of a lively wedding party in the next ward that counterpoints their own misery and intensifies the confusion of their feelings. "It was an interesting scene because the situation was that of the man telling the girl that he wanted nothing more to do with her, and to get out, and Marlon played it that way quite ruthlessly, not involving Teresa Wright at all. She was wonderful in the first two takes, but was gradually affected by his lack of response, and I had somehow to control these contradictory things—a feeling that he was freezing out the other performer, but this self-absorption absolutely fitted the character he was playing."

The relationship is also complicated by the opposition of Ellen's bourgeois family. The scene in which this is expressed is very eloquent, with the father leading off as spokesman and the mother then chiming in supportively (in other words, duplicating the male/female stereotype that Ken and Ellen will have to revise). Significantly, Ellen has to take the lead and propose to Ken.

Two—The Aftermath of War 49

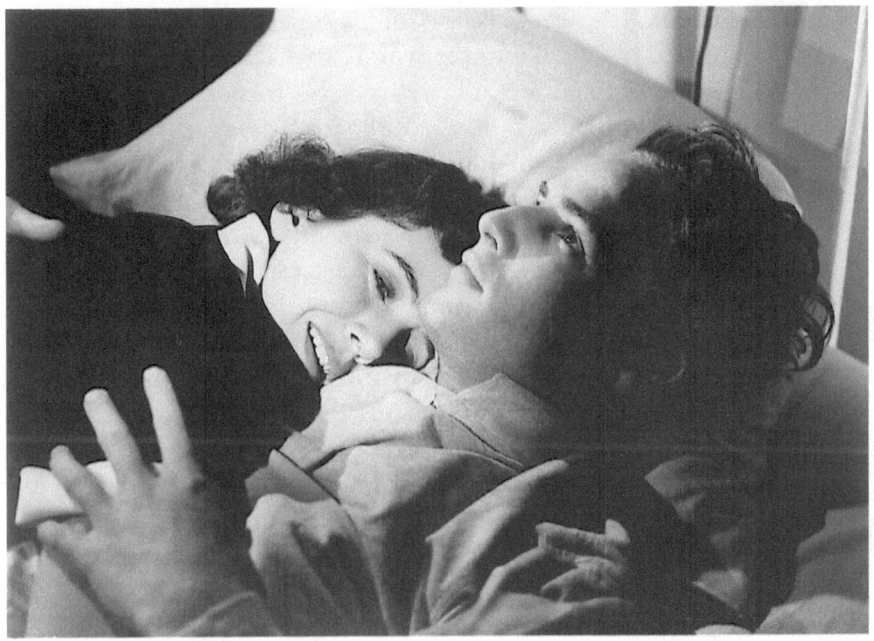

The married couple under stress in *The Men*, United Artists, 1950: Teresa Wright (left) and Marlon Brando (right).

However, the wedding scene itself is acutely uncomfortable, largely because of Ken's insistence on trying to stand during the service and only falling over. A lesser writer and director might have attempted to make something "noble" of this. In its context here, the gesture seems embarrassing, a further indication that Ken has still not come to terms with the reality of his situation. (In passing, one might note that four Zinnemann films in succession—*The Men, Teresa, High Noon* and *The Member of the Wedding*—have wedding scenes full of implications of strain and tension.) The following scene in the house is the finest in the film, partly because of its fierce charge of sexual anxiety. Ken becomes preternaturally sensitive to the noise of his wheelchair, perhaps recalling a description of a paraplegic by one of his hospital colleagues as a "freak on wheels." The tension results in a leg spasm; the almost deliberate spilling of champagne on the carpet (the sexual overtones of this are clear but emerge uninsistently and naturally from the context of the scene); and the precipitation of an argument in order not to confront the near-certainty of his sexual failure. His return to the hospital is a return to the womb, to a sanctuary from reality, to a world of men. When he returns, his friends are all watching boxing on the television, the ultimate fantasy of virility and courage which Kramer had attacked in his previous film, *Champion* (1949), and which Zinnemann was to deride in *From Here to Eternity*. The bar Ken visits subsequently with a fellow paraplegic and which leads to a fight with a customer is called, appropriately enough, The Fantasy Room. But the doctor has counselled: "Before you can change the world, you have to accept it as it is, without illusions." Ultimately the patients, against Ken's wishes, vote to discharge him from the hospital, and the doctor refuses to intervene. Ken has to return to Ellen.

The reunion at Ellen's parents is delicately done. Ken and Ellen meet outside the house—appropriately in a sort of limbo between the past they must reject and the future they must conquer. "You've come a long way," she says, a statement that has both physical and psychological overtones that are absolutely true to the spirit of the film. "Do you want me to help you up the steps?" she asks, to which he replies, "Please." This—the final word of the film—is the crucial moment when the hero accepts the reality of his dependence. The last image is a long shot, a favorite device of Zinnemann for a moment of intense emotion. Such a device respects the characters' privacy; challenges the audience's imagination; and, in this case, provides an ending that is typically unassertive and equivocal, an ending that is a question mark and a qualified beginning.

Brando's performance brings the complexity of the main character vividly to life. The struggle is an essentially private one, and Brando's very original mannerism of hesitation, peculiar speech rhythms and odd incoherences are ideal for reproducing the turbulent inner life of a troubled character. As is often the case in a Zinnemann film, the hero is not an immediately likable individual. He is sullen and stubborn. It is hard to feel sorry for someone who feels so sorry for himself. The weight of emotional involvement tends therefore to be thrown on the hero's situation more than his personality, and there are certain dimensions of this which relate to other Zinnemann concerns and go beyond simply the theme of disablement.

Firstly, the character feels trapped by his physical disability. The conception of the body as trap is to recur in *Benjy*, *A Hatful of Rain* and, to some degree, in *The Member of the Wedding*, where Frankie is always picking at herself in disgust and describing herself as a "freak." Also this sense of entrapment is to be a permanent feature of Zinnemann characters, whether they be prisoners of conscience (sometimes literally, as in *The Seventh Cross* or *A Man for All Seasons*), or characters who are unable to compromise or break free from their own sense of identity (as in, for example, *High Noon* and *From Here to Eternity*). In each case, the character has to come to terms with his or her own personality, own destiny. In each case, the process is extremely difficult, and the victory painfully won. It is this sense of difficulty which sets *The Men* apart from other "social problem" Hollywood films of the period, which tend to pose these problems in order to assert that they are all soluble. Zinnemann's films are never that assertive. They are individualistic but unlike, say, Elia Kazan's, they are about the difficulties, limits and social impotence of individualism, not the triumph. Early on, the doctor cautions Ellen against "hoping for a miracle." Miracles never happen in Fred Zinnemann: Such victories as there are have to be fought for, often alone.

It must be remembered that the title of the film is essentially ironic. These "men," in their own eyes, are hardly men at all. Dimitri Tiomkin's surging music over montages of exercise with basketball and water polo might reinforce a particularly swaggering view of active masculinity. (The music throughout is intrusive and maudlin but it is an area of the film over which Zinnemann had no control.) Yet Ken's inability to participate in games is the least of his worries. This kind of macho hero has never interested the director. "Strength" in a Zinnemann hero means psychological, not physical, strength. Ken's heroism in *The Men* comes through his ultimate refusal to take life lying down; his pulling himself upright is a reflection not of health but of an attitude to life. It also comes from his growing sense of his wife as an equal partner. Given the context in which the film was made (a few months prior to the start of the Korean War; post-war turmoil over the woman's role which reveals itself in the misogyny of film noir), the taming of the hero in the film is quite bold.

The problem with *The Men* is the one which beset *The Search*: how to alert audiences to a pressing social concern without their feeling lectured at or harrowed by the experience? How to reconcile two possible contradictory impulses in Fred Zinnemann the filmmaker: the realist and the entertainer? It is achieved mainly through conviction, craftsmanship and, just occasionally, comedy.

The camerawork is fluid and unobtrusive enough to dispel any sense of claustrophobia. As he does also in *The Nun's Story*, *Behold a Pale Horse* and *Julia*, Zinnemann elicits a lot of drama and atmosphere from the hospital setting itself, with its air of gray sterility. The players generally support Brando's superb leading performance with great sympathy and force. Teresa Wright as Ellen gives an extraordinarily sensitive performance in a difficult part. As Dr. Brock, Everett Sloane projects a volatile gruff humanity, the sense of a fiery man with something of the temperament of a Toscanini but also, more importantly, all of the dedication as well. Richard Erdman and Jack Webb as two of the patients, Leo and Norm, bring a welcome tone of toughness and humor to the ward.

Unfortunately, *The Men* did not fare too well at the box office, a fate perhaps augured by a disastrous sneak preview in San Francisco before a disappointed, restless audience that had flocked to the cinema believing they would see a preview of Ingrid Bergman in *Stromboli*. The film was released just at the start of the Korean War, and audiences were in no mood to see a film about war casualties. Nevertheless, it was a film that launched a new star, and marked an important new phase in Zinnemann's career. With one stride, he had moved a long way from MGM.

Teresa *(1951)*

As the concluding part of Zinnemann's tetralogy on post-war readjustment, *Teresa* has particular interest. It contains his most detailed reconstruction to date of actual war combat, something the previous three films allude to without extensively visualizing (Ken's crippling injury in *The Men* is all the more shocking for being so perfunctorily recorded as part of the acknowledged fringe violence of war). Also, the psychological problems of the two main characters, Philip and Teresa, relate to persistent themes in the director's career. Like so many Zinnemann protagonists, Philip has to free himself from a dependence on authority figures and find his own sense of identity. Like the boy in *The Search* and later characters in *Behold a Pale Horse*, *Julia* and *Five Days One Summer*, Teresa is made to feel physically and emotionally alien, a stranger in a foreign land. The location shooting gives a palpable sense of place that is essential for the film's purpose, for it gives conviction and nuance to the conflict of values and temperament between America and Europe, which is one of the film's main themes.

The original idea for *Teresa* had come from Arthur Loew, Sr., who, on a drive home through New York, had been struck by the hideous tenements in Brooklyn that were being erected after the war. What would happen, he thought, if a young war bride, coming to America from a war-torn Europe, found she had to live there? Alfred Hayes had done a first draft screenplay based on the idea, but no studio seemed interested. Loew showed the draft to a young writer, Stewart Stern, who had served in the U.S. Army during the war and who offered some suggestions, mainly about deepening the motivation of the main character and including combat scenes. Because of his work on *The Search* for the Loew Company, Zinnemann was a director earmarked for the project from an early stage. He had seen the Hayes draft and thought it an interesting idea (but, at that stage, too thinly developed).

Stern had met Zinnemann two years earlier. The two had been brought together by the former's intense admiration for *The Search* and the latter's liking for a Stern short story about his experiences in the war. They had worked together for two months in 1948 trying to develop a film on Israel which had become a state only a few months before and was in the midst of its first war. With Montgomery Clift, they had gone from Dan to Beer-Sheba and beyond, witnessing the action and talking to innumerable soldiers and Kibbutz people. What they saw and heard was almost impossible to compress into a film and the project was eventually abandoned. Although the outcome was frustrating, the experience, said Stern, was invaluable as an exercise in research. Stern seemed an ideal writer for *Teresa*, not only because of his first-hand knowledge of the war but because he was young enough to identify with the emotions of the young people in the story. Because Zinnemann was still editing *The Men* when *Teresa* was being planned, it was also important for him to trust someone to do the necessary research, and he knew Stern would be reliable. After all, in a way, he had taught him.

Stern was sent ahead with three particular tasks: to scout locations in Italy; to rewrite the script accordingly; and to find a leading lady. Stern followed the route of the American campaign in Italy in researching for suitable sites, at the same time advertising for leading ladies and holding auditions in Rome. He discovered an area around Mont Adone, South of Bologna, which seemed perfect. It had been the scene of fierce fighting during the war, the SS having lodged in the mountains for months. (In fact, during the film's preparation, when they were looking for uniforms, they discovered to their horror that some ex–SS men were still there, having gone underground after the war and making their living by selling left-over German military equipment, from uniforms to tanks.) The site of the bombed-out church gave Stern the idea for the wedding scene which was to be one of the highlights of the film. When the film started shooting, the war cartoonist Bill Mauldin was also involved as technical adviser and script consultant.

The casting might have been a problem but it worked out extraordinarily well. Pier Angeli as Teresa has a luminous photographic intensity (there is a wonderful close-up of her prior to entering the Cass home which catches all her mingled feelings of hope and apprehension) that no subsequent film caught with such purity. Prior to *Teresa*, she had appeared in one Italian film. Stern discovered that she had never been kissed by a man before and both he and Zinnemann attempted to deal with her feelings with the utmost sensitivity. Because of her shyness, the love scene was directed with a closed set. In his first film, John Ericson was also tremendously nervous, nevertheless (or maybe even because of this) giving a performance as Philip that has something of the tension and feeling of a James Dean. Rod Steiger, also making his screen debut as Philip's psychiatrist, froze completely when doing his first scene and could not utter his one sentence. Ralph Meeker's performance as Sergeant Dobbs is full of quiet authority: even Lee

Marvin pops up as an extra. Quite the most remarkable performance, though, is that of Patricia Collinge as Philip's possessive mother. No one who has seen the film could forget the spine-chilling moment on the beach when, seeing Philip and Teresa in deep conversation, the mother utters "S-s-secrets?," stretching the word into a sibilant hiss that seems like a spray of poison across the young couple's momentary reverie. It is a great performance because something of the pain and complexity of the mother's situation comes through as well as the spite, the moving as well as disturbing desperation of a woman looking to her son as consolation and compensation for a disappointing marriage.

Teresa begins with what is perhaps the most intimidating close-up in all of Zinnemann's work: that of an official inquiring about a claimant's employment prospects before parting with the welfare check. It is the accusatory face of bureaucracy, as seen by Philip from his vantage point of weakness of will and failure of purpose. Most significantly, the face is female, maternal, a grotesque extension of the situation at home (the dominating, questioning mother) which is at the root of Philip's problem. Later in the film, when he has a very short-lived career as a pressure-cooker salesman, he is similarly traumatized by having to demonstrate his goods to two equally intimidating mother figures. On both occasions, he runs away, sweating, the oppressive atmosphere outside corresponding to the intense pressure felt inside his own head. On the first occasion, Philip returns to his room at home. Like Ken's return to the hospital in *The Men*, the move is symbolically a return to a prison from which he must eventually escape if he is to attain maturity and fulfilment. Like Ken, he lies flat on his back—at that stage a fatalistic acceptance of his situation. The room begins to spin as a visual metaphor for the hero's swirling psychological confusion and as an introduction to the substantial flashback of Philip's war experience.

The flashback begins with a close shot of Sergeant Dobbs, who then runs towards Philip, pushing him off the path as a bomb explodes nearby. The moment is a foretaste of Dobbs' role in Philip's life as an ideal of manhood and substitute father-figure. It also suggests that Philip's forthcoming meeting with Teresa at the end of this road will be an event fraught with danger but will eventually save his life. The relationship between them develops when Philip is billeted with Teresa's family. He helps the family by trading his watch to buy them rations. In exchanging a gift from his mother for food to help the Italian family, he signals a subconscious desire to free himself from his mother's grip because of his developing love for Teresa.

The romance is interrupted by approaching danger and the men are ordered to go on patrol. They tensely advance in a twilight procession towards the enemy. At one moment, there is a high-pitched nerve-tingling screech and Philip is told by Dobbs that "some animal stepped on a mine." It is never definitely established whether this is true or not, but the sound lingers, as an example of the director's mastery at conveying a world of horror through a heightened use of sound. (The torture scenes of *The Seventh Cross* and *The Day of the Jackal* are similarly indicated and are correspondingly chilling.) The noise lingers for another reason. It purposely anticipates the most blood-curdling moment in the film: the later hysterical screech of Philip's mother, like that of a wounded animal, when she, metaphorically speaking, is to step on a mine—that is, to discover the photograph of her son's marriage.

Camping by a stream, Philip begins to shiver from cold and fear, and Dobbs gives him his scarf. Like the jacket in *Act of Violence*, the tin star in *High Noon*, the jam jar in *The Sundowners*, the Chancellor's chain of office in *A Man for All Seasons*, the scarf is an object that gathers cumulative meaning in the film's structure. Dobbs is to be killed in the attack, partly because Philip panics and cries out. The scarf is then treasured by Philip both as a souvenir of an ideal and as a reminder of his sense of failure and responsibility for the man's death.

After the battle experience, Philip returns to Teresa. Their wedding is one of the most remarkable scenes in all of Zinnemann's work, the ceremony being enacted on a windy day in a bombed-out church against a vivid mountain background. This setting is beautiful, bizarre and wonderfully expressive. It suggests the incompleteness of the personalities being united; anticipates the storms to come; indicates the potential of new life emerging from the rubble of war; and conveys the sense of the frailty of humanity when set against imperious Nature. A lively montage of their

Italian honeymoon follows, which is cut short by a shot of an empty Italian square, the cessation of the festive music, and a slow reverse tracking shot (like a withdrawal of the soul into the self) as Philip stands at the window and tells Teresa he has to return to America. The shot of Philip framed in the window foretells his feeling of entrapment in America and indeed anticipates a series of shots later where he is to be seen framed in shadow in a doorway or a room, boxed in, barred, with his wife waiting on one side of the image while the mother calls out to him from the other. There is a lovely moment when Teresa insists that Philip say "I love you" in Italian—a more romantic language but also an omen of their difficulty in expressing their love on American soil. The scene is imbued with the sense of painful farewell that is to be something of a Zinnemann hallmark (there are similarly heart-rending separations in *The Search, High Noon, The Nun's Story, Julia* and *Five Days One Summer*).

Philip's return home is oppressively gloomy. As he climbs the stairs of the tenement building in which he lives, the sounds of family bickering drift through the walls, a foretaste of the domestic tension he will face. (A similar scene occurs in *The Member of the Wedding*, when Frankie has her unpleasant encounter with that adult world.) For a moment, Philip hesitates, on one of Zinnemann's most dramatically charged staircases. Indeed, he turns away, afraid to go in, a reminder of the narrator's comment on Philip with which the film opened ("His name is Philip Cass. His occupation—running away").

The welcoming is finely characterized. His sister (Peggy Ann Garner) greets Philip with great joy, and his mother is exited to the point of near-hysteria. The reaction of his mild-mannered father (Richard Bishop) is photographed with great sensitivity. Overcome, he leans forward in shadow as if to kiss his son, at which Philip recoils in embarrassment and his father's head jerks back into the light, a harsh glare suddenly thrown onto his feeling of discomfort. Later that night, when Philip has not said anything of Teresa, his mother enters his bedroom and he pretends to be asleep. It is a neat scene, conveying character in a gesture (the mother's concern for her son revealed by the way she stops the chair from rocking so that the noise will not wake him). It also picks up the motif of pretending to be asleep which recurs several times in the film, as if the characters are people who do not want to wake up, to move into maturity, to face reality. Teresa does it as a joke on her wedding night, a touching portrait of a "sleeping beauty" prior to the loss of her innocence. For Philip, the gesture is his mode of evasion, closing his eyes to problems in the hope that they disappear rather than confront them through an act of will. One might say that he enters the state of matrimony with his eyes shut, deliberately closing his mind to the problems his marriage will create at home. His mother has to discover about Teresa for herself.

Teresa and Philip are reunited in a remarkable war-brides scene, where soldiers and wives (and sometimes babies) are lined up at opposite sides of the quay, names are called, and wives are claimed as if lost property—which, in a way, is what they are. The scene is shot in such a way that one is made aware of the expanse of empty space between the couples and the long distance they have to travel to reach each other. It's an image that suggests both a union across two continents but also the immense distance these people will have to travel in order to make the marriage work. Teresa instantly feels alienated by the Cass family atmosphere, so different from that of her own family. Her welcoming compares interestingly with that of Philip's homecoming: the sister again friendly; Teresa making a move of affection towards the father which Philip checks; the mother having to be brought out of her room to greet her daughter-in-law. It does not take Teresa long to sense the contending claims of the mother for Philip's love. One sign of this struggle is their different manner of addressing him: "Philipo" from Teresa (a recollection of the man she fell in love with in Italy), "Sonny" from his mother (a name that asserts her matriarchal claims on his affections, insists that he is still her child). If he has been exhausted by the domestic strain, so too has Teresa. She begins to shake when he goes out for a job that may mean freedom for them, in the same way he used to shake when going into battle. When she becomes pregnant and realizes Philip has neither the will nor seemingly the inclination to break out of his family situation, she leaves.

The final part of the film perhaps resolves things a little too easily. Philip finally finds enough courage to leave home and his father finds sufficient self-assertion to prevent his mother from stopping him. Philip and his father are reconciled at the hospital when Philip learns he is a father (no need to comment on the gift from Dad of a box of cigars!) and Philip and Teresa are also reconciled and find a new apartment. It should be noted, however, that the last scene in the bare flat is rather reminiscent of that empty Italian square and that vast space on the New York quayside where husbands and their foreign wives were reunited: They might be making a fresh start but they still have a long way to travel.

Much of the credit for the film must go to Stewart Stern, whose screenplay seems, on one level, a fascinating rehearsal for his subsequent scenario for *Rebel Without a Cause*, with its young hero tormented by a weak, castrated father and a shrill, tigerish mother. The blend of personality between writer and director makes for a compelling, rewarding tension. Stern has talked of his early tendency to write too much in terms of emotional climaxes and the value of working with directors like Zinnemann and Paul Newman (on *Rachel, Rachel*) who like to hold such climaxes back. Conversely, there is a visual exuberance and ornateness to the film that one does not ordinarily associate with Zinnemann, but which is the fascinating product of finding the appropriate style for so emotionally dynamic a script.

Zinnemann and Stern were subsequently to work together on a short film, *Benjy* (1951). This came about when Zinnemann's wife was being treated in a hospital with a broken leg and the doctor who attended her revealed that he was in charge of a children's hospital in Los Angeles that was desperately short of funds. Fred offered to make a fund-raising film. Stern agreed to write it and did his usual first-hand research, dressing up as a doctor for two weeks and talking to the children and doctors before fashioning the moving story of *Benjy*, which was to win an Oscar as the best short of the year.

With *Teresa*, Zinnemann had come to a turning point in his development. It is a work of stylistic and thematic transition. It invigoratingly combines documentary austerity with ornate and extravagant imagery (as in the wedding scene). It looks back to the war and forward to the American present. By the end of *Teresa*,

Zinnemann had said all he needed to say about the problems of veterans in post-war America. He could now say something about the equally urgent problems confronting the individual in Cold War America. He chose to say it in the form of a Western—one of the most famous Westerns ever made.

CHAPTER THREE

Character Is Destiny

High Noon *(1952)*

> An idea that has meant a lot to me is Robert Louis Stevenson's: "A man's character is his destiny." It is the theme of some of my most successful films.
> —Fred Zinnemann

High Noon is one of those films which has been all things to all men: classic Western, Greek morality play, political allegory. Studio politics as much as contemporary politics influenced its final outcome, and although much has been read into the film in retrospect (both for and against), it started out as a modest film about a compelling moral dilemma.

At the outset, Stanley Kramer, writer Carl Foreman and Zinnemann agreed that *High Noon* was a Western only incidentally. For Foreman, the story was basically that of a town corrupted by fear. In his eyes, particularly after his appearance before the House of Un-American Activities Committee and his blacklisting for his refusal either to confirm or deny his affiliation with the Communist Party, the community in the story was a symbol of Hollywood. For Zinnemann, the theme was not contemporary but timeless: a story of conscience. Although framed by a suspenseful exposition and a vividly exciting final shoot-out, the heart of the film is in the anguished central section when each member of the town finds his or her very plausible reason for not coming to the aid of a man who needs help.

Unlike the usual Western, *High Noon* has no daunting landscapes and comparatively little action. Also, the Marshal is not a superhero. One is constantly aware of his vulnerability. It is characteristic that Zinnemann would approach a genre like the Western, with its accretions of escapism, fantasy and myth, from the perspective of realism: It is what gave the film its originality then and preserves its interest now. Whereas directors like Anthony Mann and John Sturges created their Western drama from the tension between man and landscape, Zinnemann creates his tension from close-ups of Gary Cooper's lined face.

In aiming for realism, Zinnemann was fortunate to have as cameraman Floyd Crosby, a man and technician for whom he had the highest admiration. Much of Crosby's experience had been gained through collaborating with some of the greatest documentary filmmakers. He had worked with F.W. Murnau and Robert Flaherty on *Tabu* (1931), with Pare Lorentz on *The River* (1937) and Joris Ivens on *Power and the Land* (1940). He and Zinnemann agreed that *High Noon* should have the look of an old newsreel, if such a thing had existed at the end of the last century. The film should have a grainy, deglamorized look that was quite unlike the inspiring expanses of most Westerns. The studio chiefs were horrified when they saw the rushes, and a lesser man might have succumbed to their pressure. Crosby stuck to his guns. His photography is essential to the film's effect and tone. It not only conveys a convincing impression of what the Old West must have been like: its deliberate flatness somehow seems to mirror the inertia of the townspeople. At the same time, the film is a photographic *tour de force*. Few who have seen *High Noon* will have forgotten the moment when the Marshal has to face the outlaws alone and the camera cranes until he is seen as a tiny figure on an absolutely deserted street. Paradoxically, in pulling the camera away from the character at this point, the film seems to involve an audience all the more in his isolation and despair.

Three—Character Is Destiny

A further dimension of Zinnemann's realistic approach was the casting of Gary Cooper as the Marshal. He needed someone of sufficient star stature who could involve and sustain an audience's sympathy: Cooper's extraordinary screen charisma ensured that. At the same time, he needed someone who could reveal a touching, human fallibility. Perhaps because of his illness prior to the shooting of the film, Cooper looks tired and drawn, emphasized still more by Zinnemann's typical insistence on a minimum of makeup. No attempt is made to disguise the actor's true age, which adds to the feeling of poignancy. The hero *is* tired (in this regard, *High Noon* is the forerunner of a number of key Westerns of the '60s, such as *Ride the High Country*, *The Man Who Shot Liberty Valance* and *The Wild Bunch*, which play on the Western hero as a heroic but ageing anachronism). Marshal Kane is now weary of this kind of struggle, thinking he had seen the end of it and believing that the taming of the wilderness had at last been achieved. It makes it that much harder for him to turn and face again the danger. His marriage to a much younger woman (rather like the marriage of the Van Heflin character in *Act of Violence*) seems almost a symbolic gesture: a conscious desire to make a fresh start, the woman's Quaker religion an additional attraction—it is almost a projection of *his* desire for peace. Because of this, the return to confrontation is all the more difficult and painful, and the progression of the film ensures that his perspiration, exhaustion and self-doubts are brought home very powerfully.

While using realism as his overall stylistic base, Zinnemann also had a precise visual schema in his mind while shooting the film. He decided that the menace should be presented statically: Once the three outlaws have established themselves at the depot for the arrival of their leader, they should stay there, more or less motionless, for the next hour. (One of them goes briefly into the town, but does not stay long.) There would be no shots of Miller on the train, approaching the town. The threat would be conveyed entirely by shots of the tracks, from where the danger was to come. Set across this static menace would be the constant movement of the Marshal in the town, compelled to cover practically the whole area in order to try (unavailingly) to elicit support. People will not let him into their homes, and he must remain, rather as the John

Gary Cooper in his most famous role as the Marshal too proud to run when four outlaws come seeking revenge. From *High Noon*, United Artists, 1952.

Wayne character will remain in Ford's *The Searchers* (1956), outside in the wilderness, compelled to deal alone with what the "civilized" people feel is a Westerner's problem.

A further conscious strategy of Zinnemann's and Foreman's was the highlighting of the awareness of time. Like the action of the film, time is moving slowly but inexorably toward its dramatic climax. As the time factor begins to loom larger in the Marshal's mind, so the close-ups of the clocks themselves grow larger, more menacing. It gathers to the point where, as noon approaches, the pendulum of the clock in the Marshal's office swings slowly, in an almost hallucinatory fashion, as a Poe-like instrument of execution. (One of the myths about the making of the film is that these shots of the clocks were added by editor Elmo Williams to heighten tension. In fact, Williams told me that, on the contrary, these shots were not only already there but limited his own room for maneuver, for they very precisely indicated the time passage of the film.)

Other visual strategies were also precisely planned by the director. It was decided that the Marshal should wear a black waist-coat over a white shirt, enabling him to stand out visually against the white sky and thereby highlighting his isolation. (The white sky was most obligingly supplied by the smog on the Columbia back lot in San Fernando Valley.) Subliminally, too, the costuming seems to link him to the two women in his life: the shirt a reminder of his wife, Amy (Grace Kelly), who is throughout dressed in white; the waist-coat evoking Helen (Katy Jurado), his former mistress, who is throughout dressed in black. It is a clever way of keeping to the forefront of our consciousness the tensions at war within the Marshal—between past and present, passion and peace. This tension is perhaps most powerfully felt through the symbolic weight given to two objects in the film; the Marshal's tin star (the symbol of Federal authority which he represents and is responsible to) and Amy's wedding ring (the symbol of promise for his future).

The star and the ring are very prominent in the film's famous finale. The wedding ring is in the foreground of the frame when the two embrace (representing the future that the Marshal can now embrace). The tin star, in the Marshal's memorable gesture of contempt for the community, is thrown into the dust, leaving the town without a leader and facing an uncertain future. The Marshal has retained his self-respect, but the residue of bitterness is the recognition that he has preserved a town not worth saving. The bitterness of this ending is perhaps presaged in that remarkable early scene when the Marshal, to his surprise, discovers that the Judge is leaving town. He has heard of the threat to the town and, while packing his things, warns the Marshal of what will happen. The things he packs are his law books, his scales of justice and the American flag—law, justice and American ideals being precisely the things that are to be "packed up" when this situation develops. For those who read the film allegorically as about Hollywood and McCarthyist America, the symbolism of this scene is especially forceful.

Strong stuff for a Western, then, and with a working team of such strong-minded professionals as Zinnemann, Foreman, Crosby, producer Stanley Kramer, composer Dimitri Tiomkin and editor Elmo Williams, it was inevitable that some points of contention would arise during the development of the project. The contentious elements in this case were undoubtedly aggravated by two factors: Carl Foreman's investigation by the HUAC which necessitated his departure from the film halfway through its shooting; and the film's preview, which convinced many that the film would be a disaster.

Both Kramer and Elmo Williams felt that Zinnemann had given too much prominence to the Grace Kelly part, and that a certain readjustment of emphasis was needed in her scenes with Katy Jurado. At the editing stage, Williams also eliminated a subplot involving a deputy who is due back to help the Marshal and who does not arrive in time. However, in an interview in *American Film* (April 1979), Carl Foreman indicated that the subplot was only an insurance against an audience's feeling too constricted by the concentration on the Marshal and would probably have been eliminated anyway. (Zinnemann never liked the idea of a subplot because he was trying for unity of time and place, and could never recall shooting these scenes.) "To say that a lot of footage was unusable," Foreman continues in this interview, "is a vicious libel against Fred Zinnemann, the director, who did such a magnificent job. Had I been in the country when the picture came out.... I can assure you that this very big lie would never have been allowed to be told and grow." Whatever the personality conflicts involved (and these were considerable), everyone to whom I spoke about *High Noon* dismissed as absurd the hurtful myth that the original cut of the film was inadequate and that the film was rescued in the editing room. Elmo Williams described that story to me as "bullshit," and Stanley Kramer said he thought Zinnemann had done a "brilliant job."

No one would dispute the importance of Dimitri Tiomkin's music to the film. The ballad (with lyrics by Ned Washington) supplies an element of folk-tale to the material. While keeping the wife in the foreground of our mind and then helping to amplify sympathy for the Marshal, the ballad also serves as a valuable dramatic monologue, putting into words what the Marshal feels but cannot articulate for himself. Not all of Tiomkin's musical cues were to be found in the final film (Kramer said he eliminated about five) and Tiomkin seemed to be initially resistant about the style required. Williams told me that, for Tiomkin, he suggested a style along the lines of "Ghost Riders in the Sky": for lyricist Ned Washington, a dignified poetic style along the lines of Carl Sandburg's *Chicago* poems. There were some disagreements among the personnel when Zinnemann had left the picture after completing the first cut. For example, the editor wanted no music but a heightened use of soundtrack to convey the tension of the few minutes immediately preceding the arrival of the noon train—the scratching of Kane's pen, the ticking of the clock, a sudden, unnaturally loud shriek of the train whistle—but he was overruled by composer and producer. In the event, everything worked out well.

The moral of this is simply that, like all films, *High Noon* was basically a team effort. Nevertheless, more than any film prior to this, it did serve to bring into focus certain themes and conflicts that were to recur insistently in Zinnemann's films and life. It elaborated a characteristic Zinnemann protagonist: a loner with a strong sense of duty who knows he could not live with himself if he were to go against his conscience. There is no choice for him: The Marshal in *High Noon* acts in the manner he does not because it is his job but because it is what he is. "I'm the same man, with or without this," he says of the tin star. He is locked inside his own character, unable to justify it other than by action. ("If you don't know, I can't explain" is a recurrent refrain in *High Noon*, and indicates the difficulty of any comprehension between people whose lives are based on principle and those whose lives are based on survival.)

His indomitable will, as we shall see, is to be a feature also of the main characters of *From Here to Eternity*, *The Nun's Story* and *A Man for All Seasons*. It should be emphasized that these characters are not set up as one-dimensional moral exemplars. "To be human at all, we must stand fast a little, *even at the risk* of being heroes," says More in *A Man for All Seasons*. Yet, as someone said ironically of T.E. Lawrence, they are invariably, if unwittingly, "backing into the limelight." This is not to undermine the courage of what they do, but rather to indicate the maturity and complexity that is demanded of an audience in responding to them, which is far removed from the easy identification conferred on the conventional Hollywood hero.

Such characters also make life very difficult for others, in *High Noon* and *A Man for All Seasons* provoking even their wives to temporary rebellion and hatred. They exasperate and antagonize people, both people who wish to help them (like Norfolk in *A Man for All Seasons*) and others whose fun is being spoiled by their presence (like that oily hotel clerk in *High Noon*). One of the striking things about *High Noon* is the number of people who dislike the Marshal, who feel he's got a "comeuppance" coming. It is as if he forces people to confront the inadequacies and weaknesses within themselves. By standing fast, he compels others to take sides where they would prefer to abdicate or compromise. For a Zinnemann hero, there are things worse than death. The converse of that is represented by the townspeople in *High Noon*, who, like some of the people the fugitive encounters in *The Seventh Cross*, like Enley in *Act of Violence*, will do, or refuse to do, anything to save their own skin. If *High Noon* is, on one level, about the conscience of the Marshal, it is also about the tragedy of a town. What price do people put on stability, peace, appeasement? When will they stand up to evil?

These themes are universal. Nevertheless, the atmosphere in McCarthyist America, the fate of Carl Foreman, must have sharpened them. They were also certainly sharpened in Zinnemann's mind by his memory of the famous Screen Directors Guild meeting of October 1950, when Cecil B. DeMille and his faction tried unsuccessfully to have Joseph L. Mankiewicz deposed as President of the Guild. Zinnemann had been one of the 25 signatories to a petition calling for this urgent General Meeting "to consider the proposed recall of the President." The meeting was ostensibly about Joseph Mankiewicz's Presidency. It was actually all part of

DeMille's attempt to root out "Communism" in the American film industry by whatever means, and the meeting turned into a free-ranging discussion about free speech, democracy and the Constitution of the United States. Zinnemann told me he remembered the night as "one of the most extraordinary of my life, a night in which people were really compelled to stick their necks out for what they believed in." (One certainly wonders what might have happened to the careers of those twenty-five signatories if the DeMille faction, and not that of Mankiewicz, had won the argument.) Something of the intensity of that night, however subconsciously, seeps into that scene in the church in *High Noon*, which has the atmosphere of a debate and in which everyone crucially has his or her say. In the Mankiewicz-DeMille fracas, the crucial intervention came late on from a handkerchief-chewing John Ford who declared he made Westerns, complimented DeMille as a filmmaker before denouncing him as a man, and urging that they give Mankiewicz their support and get back to work. In *High Noon*, the crucial intervention comes late on from a handkerchief-waving, John Ford regular, Thomas Mitchell, who compliments the Marshal as a man, before denouncing his tactics on what one might call political grounds, and effectively withdrawing his (and the townspeople's) support. With all the contempt he can muster, with that understatement and the terrifyingly controlled anger which is part of the Zinnemann hero and the Fred Zinnemann character, the Marshal responds with just one word: a withering "Thanks."

High Noon ends bitterly, and there was bitterness in its making, but its destiny was an unexpectedly happy one. It was a runaway commercial success, and for many critics the film of the year. Zinnemann was voted best director by the New York critics, but, although nominated for the Hollywood Oscar, he lost out to John Ford with *The Quiet Man*. But he did not have long to wait.

From Here to Eternity *(1953)*

> When he finished packing, he walked out onto the third-floor porch of the barracks brushing the dust from his hands, a very neat and deceptively slim young man in the summer khakis that were still early morning fresh.
> —James Jones, *From Here to Eternity*, Chapter 1

It was from this description of Prewitt in the novel ("very neat and deceptively slim") that Fred Zinnemann first had his idea of casting Montgomery Clift. Once he had that image in his mind, he could not shake it. Maybe Prewitt had been a boxer, and Monty Clift did not look like an ex-boxer, but the boxing aspect did not interest Zinnemann at all. "The crisis was one of principle: Prewitt would not box for his new Army barracks because he had blinded his opponent in his last bout, and no amount of pressure, physical or mental, would shift him." More than any other young actor of the time, Clift was superbly equipped to convey that sense of stubbornness. Uniquely among actors of that time, he could express inner strength, his eyes as much as his actions flaming rebellion. Prewitt's stand could just have been one of several sources of dramatic conflict in the tale. With Clift, as Zinnemann intended, it becomes the central theme. However, Zinnemann's insistence on this brought him into conflict with Columbia's notorious studio head, Harry Cohn.

Cohn was staking much of his own personal status on *From Here to Eternity*. When he had bought the film rights of the novel, the property had been known as "Cohn's Folly," because no one thought that the book's sex and violence and its anti–Army slant could be brought into screen shape. (This was shortly after the Korean War and Senator McCarthy was still going strong. The American Army was still what it had been since 1940—an almost sacred institution.) After a number of unsuccessful attempts, including one by the book's author, James Jones, Daniel Taradash wrote a treatment which seemed to solve all the problems. The sex could be implied rather than shown, partly by calling Prewitt's girlfriend Lorene (Donna Reed) a "hostess" rather than a prostitute and by making the place a "club" rather than a brothel; and partly by suggesting the passion shared by Sergeant Warden (Burt Lancaster) and the wife of his Commanding Officer, Karen (Deborah Kerr), rather than showing it in detail (the famous beach scene with its surging tide). The harsher elements of the novel could be retained but expressed in an indirect rather than explicit manner. For example, the inside of the military prison is not shown (all we see is Fatso Judson's back and the way he holds his truncheon as Maggio is marched towards him, and that is enough).

But Maggio's fate in the film—he is killed whereas in the novel, he is only badly hurt—epitomizes the sadism of the stockade. Also the sprawling structure of the novel could be tightened by a judicious paralleling of events.

The novel seemed to have been mastered for the screen. Also the producer Buddy Adler, who had been a Lieutenant-Colonel in World War Two, seemed to have ensured the cooperation of the Army. As it happened, the Army liked the script so much that they did not wish to harm it. But they made two conditions for their cooperation: that the inside of the stockade should not be shown; and that the fate of the villainous Captain Holmes should be changed from book to film. In the book he is promoted to the rank of Major. In the film he is reprimanded and given the choice of resigning or facing a court-martial. He resigns (in the weakest scene of the film). These conditions were accepted, for it was felt that, without the Army's cooperation, it would have been impossible to make a credible and authentic film about professional soldiers.

Both Taradash and Buddy Adler pressed the claim of Zinnemann to direct the film. "I had seen *Teresa*," recalled Taradash to me, "and I thought it had the best-portrayed soldiers I can remember seeing on the screen at that time, and I thought Fred would be a hell of a director for *From Here to Eternity*." Cohn at first seemed to waver, understandably so. He had staked a lot of his personal reputation on *From Here to Eternity*, and Zinnemann at that time was regarded as something of an "art house" director, gifted but with a limited following. At this stage, *High Noon*, his first big commercial success, had not yet been released. Cohn had seen a cutting print of it and had handed it back to Kramer with the words: "Who cares? It's a piece of junk." (Later, when working together on *From Here to Eternity*, Zinnemann enjoyed torturing Cohn by reminding him of how much money he had thrown out of the window.)

Cohn and Zinnemann met and, for all their disagreements, developed a wary but genuine respect for each other. "He had little education, not much taste, but a gut instinct for good showmanship," said Zinnemann. "He was a very enthusiastic man who was deeply distrustful of people in general and was always looking for someone to say No to him, and mean it. He could be unbelievably rude. If he thought people were scared of him, he went

The famous beach scene in *From Here to Eternity*, Columbia Pictures, 1953: Burt Lancaster and Deborah Kerr.

for the jugular. I very quickly discovered his weak points. It had to do with money always. I won a good many battles and lost quite a few."

Two examples of Cohn's "weakness" about money were to prove significant for the film. Part of his objection to Montgomery Clift in the leading role was Cohn's desire to cast a Columbia contract player, Aldo Ray, as Prewitt. The actor had not worked for ten weeks while being paid a good salary and Cohn was anxious to put a halt to a situation where a man was being paid for doing nothing. Also, Cohn wanted someone who looked like a boxer; Zinnemann wanted someone who could convey the feeling that his spirit could not be broken. After a memorable battle ("I am the President of Columbia, you can't give me ultimatums"), Cohn finally gave in and sent the script to Clift.

The casting of Frank Sinatra as Maggio also came about indirectly through a clash over money. Zinnemann and Taradash had both agreed that Eli Wallach was the best man for the role. According to Taradash, Wallach's agent then suggested a fee to Cohn that was much higher than the latter had envisaged, and when Cohn was pressed for an urgent reply because Wallach had an alternative offer to appear in Tennessee Williams' *Camino Real* on stage under Elia Kazan, Cohn insisted that Wallach was to be released. There was no way Cohn would tolerate being pressured over money.

At that time, Sinatra was with Ava Gardner in Nairobi, where John Ford was shooting *Mogambo*, but at Cohn's request he flew back at his own expense to make a test which turned out to be good. "We looked at the test," Taradash told me, "and a funny thing happened. The scene was the one where Maggio gets drunk and strips to the waist and hot-headedly picks a fights with two military policemen. Wallach acted the scene superbly but, when he stripped to the waist, he looked pretty robust, well able to take care of himself, and the scene really elicited no sympathy. When Sinatra stripped to the waist, he looked so scrawny that your heart went out to this little guy being picked on by two M.P.s. It was then we thought it might work and in the end, of course, we were very lucky, because Sinatra was wonderful in the picture." Sinatra was paid a thousand dollars a week for eight weeks, which was a modest fee even in those days. But the film transformed his career, winning him an Oscar.

The two other main parts to be cast were the women. The key to the character of the "hostess," Lorene, Zinnemann thought, was her nickname, "Princess." It was not simply that she did not conform to the usual idea of a prostitute. It was also that the character was basically a *bourgeois*, wanting to earn enough money to become the classiest lady of her distant home town. With that concept in mind, the elegant and refined Donna Reed was cast and brought out the character's complexities exceptionally well. As for the role of Karen Holmes, the Captain's wife, Joan Crawford was originally proposed, but the idea met with little enthusiasm from Zinnemann and the team. It was agent Bert Allenberg who proposed Deborah Kerr, provoking the derision of Cohn but immediately intriguing Zinnemann, Adler and Taradash, who found it a fascinating idea. Zinnemann always liked casting against type.

"If Clift was unusual casting as a boxer and Donna Reed as a prostitute, even more so was Deborah Kerr as a nymphomaniac. Previously she had hardly played anything but cool English rose types. But if you cast against type, you challenge the actor or actress to bring out new facets of his or her personality and, because it's not what they expect, the audiences become more curious about and more involved with the character." Kerr's performance conveys genuine passion and anguish underneath the ostensible poise.

There were some final, small refinements to be made to the screenplay, in which everyone otherwise had the utmost confidence. "Unlike some directors I've worked with," Taradash told me, "Fred was not a frustrated writer, but he was good at putting his finger on a weakness in a scene. For example, originally the scene where Lorene tells Prewitt that her real name is Alma Burke took place on the beach and was a throwaway detail. Fred felt there was something wrong there, that the film stopped at that point. In making me re-think that moment, shifting the setting of it and giving it an edge of conflict, I think he improved the scene enormously." Taradash had a similar experience with Harry Cohn. Mostly the script conferences consisted of Cohn's unsuccessful attempts to breach the united front of Taradash, Zinnemann and Adler: It was his way of testing whether they believed in the project as much as he did. Although many of his ideas were terrible, some were good, and he could be very obstinate. He insisted to Taradash that, as Prewitt was supposed to be a great bugler, he ought to demonstrate this ability early in the film. Taradash's argument was that it was better to keep the audience in suspense until the moment when he plays "Taps" as a tribute to his dead friend, Maggio. But Cohn persisted and, after racking his brains, Taradash came up with that moment in the bar when Prewitt snatches the bugle from a young soldier and improvizes a dazzling jazz arrangement of "Chatanooga Choo Choo." It is very effective, a startling sense of release from a character who has been oppressed almost from the first moment of the film, and a hint of an inner gaiety and freedom in Prewitt which rarely finds a means of expression. One or two scenes which both Zinnemann and Taradash wished to remain in the script—a scene where the men sing "Re-enlistment Blues" and another where they discuss old movie stars, both

Woman trouble: Sgt. Leva (Mickey Shaughnessy, center) and Sgt. Warden (Burt Lancaster) warily observe the wife of their commanding officer, Karen Holmes (Deborah Kerr), who has a reputation for promiscuity.

scenes from the novel—were omitted at Cohn's insistence, because he was adamant that the film should not be longer than two hours. It finally ran 118 minutes.

The film was brought in on a tight shooting schedule of seven weeks, and, from its first screening, immediately proved to be one of the most highly acclaimed and financially successful films in the history of Columbia Pictures. The film had started shooting on March 1, 1953, and opened only five months later in August, in the Capitol Theatre, New York. Zinnemann had vivid memories of the opening. "It was the first time that a 'big' film opened in summer and people thought Cohn was mad. These were the days before air conditioning and New York was as hot as a steambath. Moreover Cohn insisted there would be no advance publicity, except for one full-page ad in *The New York Times,* signed by him as president of Columbia in which he recommended the film. On the night of the opening, I was in L.A., just going to bed, when a phone call came from Marlene Dietrich in New York, saying that the theater was bulging and there were lines around the block. It was not past midnight in New York. 'How is that possible? There has been no publicity,' I said. 'They smell it,' she replied."

The opening shot is an exposition of the film's main theme, condensing the first 50 pages of the novel into a single image. A soldier, Robert E. Lee Prewitt, walks slowly towards the camera from the background of the shot as a troop of soldiers, doing drill, march across the foreground of the frame. It sets up an immediate conflict between the individual and the group and between the purposeful path of one man and the rigid uniformity of a regulated Army machine. With the soldiers marching across Prewitt's line of approach, the shot is an omen of Prewitt's destruction by his conflict with that kind of discipline. It is a classic instance of bringing information simply and concisely to the camera. Some years earlier, John Ford had told Zinnemann, in a spirit of friendly advice: "You move the camera too goddamn much. Think of the camera as an information booth." (When Joe Mankiewicz was asked how people would know when John Ford's section begins in *How the West Was Won*, Mankiewicz replied: "It'll be when the camera is still.") The opening shot of *From Here to Eternity* is the one which best demonstrates Zinnemann's individual use of that advice.

From Here to Eternity shows the influence of Ford in several other marginal details. The knife fight between Prewitt and Judson (Ernest Borgnine), who is responsible for the death of Prewitt's friend, Maggio, is done obliquely and in shadow. The suspense that accrues from this and the momentary apprehension that Judson has won as he staggers into camera range before collapsing, recalls Ford's similar staging of the final gunfight and its outcome in *Stagecoach*. The tenderness of the "Taps" sequence—the music drifting out over the barracks and touching every man who hears it, bringing them all into momentary union—has something of the feeling of the campfire song sequences of Ford's cavalry film, *Rio Grande* (1950). (During the Pearl Harbor sequence, the bugler in the barracks gets so excited that he inadvertently starts blowing a

cavalry charge.) The film's ambivalent attitude to the Army has the kind of tension between recognition of the need for discipline yet a desire to see that discipline imposed with understanding and humanity that informs a film like Ford's *Fort Apache* (1948). "How can you love the Army when it treats you so badly?" Lorene asks Prewitt at one stage. "Just because you love something doesn't mean it has to love you back," Prewitt replies. "I left home at 17. I didn't belong no place until I joined the Army." The Army is his home—and it destroys him. "Home" is invariably a precarious concept in Zinnemann's films, where security and a sense of belonging have either to be fought for or are suddenly undermined.

The characterization has recognizable traits from the gallery of situations that particularly seem to stimulate Zinnemann's interest in a subject. Burt Lancaster's observant performance as Sergeant Warden has his usual kinetic energy but also a measure of detachment and watchfulness, reflecting Warden as a careful man who calculates every step. Just as the affair with Karen Holmes is conducted with the meticulousness of an undercover military operation, so is his army life conducted with the minimum of risk and the refusal to stick his neck out too far. He will not get into a fight unless he is absolutely certain he can win it, or (as in the case of his confrontation with Judson) he knows the other person will back off. It is the difference between him and Prewitt, who is forever banging his head against a brick wall. It is the reason that he will not support hotheads like Prewitt and Maggio, however he might secretly sympathize with them. Warden will not go up against an institution. In contrast, Maggio is over-emotional, allows his heart to rule his head, and seems always running into trouble. Irrespective of the institution, Prewitt stubbornly refuses to give ground because of what he believes. "If a man don't go his own way, he's nothing...," he says.

Prewitt is "one against the world." In several images of the film he is seen claustrophobically surrounded by people who are barring his exit (the scene in Captain Holmes' office, or the scene around the pool table) and who each want him to behave in a particular way. "You're expected to play ball," he is told, a line that seems to resonate as a vision of life, of society that must be resisted. "They're gonna get you sooner or later," he is also told, the character in a

Private Maggio (Frank Sinatra, center) comes to the defense of his friend Prewitt (Montgomery Clift, left) when he is persecuted by Sgt. Henderson (Robert Wilke).

"no escape" situation that is often the lot of the Zinnemann protagonist. Everyone tries to blackmail him into betraying his principles. Even Lorene says she will marry him if he goes to America with her and leaves the Army. His stand of principle makes others feel uneasy. Although Prewitt is often seen with a pack on his back, it is he who is a burden to those with whom he comes into contact. His individualism forces others into some uncomfortable situations and decisions.

At the end of *From Here to Eternity*, Pearl Harbor has made the ideology of one man seem suddenly irrelevant in the national concern, and Prewitt is accidentally killed by a nervous guard on his way back to the camp. When Warden crouches over Prewitt's dead body on the beach, he tells him softly that boxing is to be dropped from the routine of the barracks anyway. So Prewitt's stand of principle, objectively speaking, was ultimately pointless.

When Karen and Lorene meet unexpectedly for the first time in a beautifully played final scene on the boat taking them back to America, Lorene has already invented an explanation for Prewitt's death that builds him up to be among the many dead of the first day of war and conforms to a more conventional concept of heroism.

So what has Prewitt achieved? What do any of these Fred Zinnemann characters actually accomplish? In the terms of the conventional Hollywood cinema, not a great deal—and, in some ways, that is precisely where the originality of these films lies. It is hard to speculate where the Marshal will go at the end of *High Noon* or what the nun will do at the end of *The Nun's Story*, and the unwavering convictions of Prewitt in *From Here to Eternity* and More in *A Man for All Seasons* lead directly to their graves. But they have stayed on the path that is their concept of their destiny. In personal terms, that is their triumph, because it vindicates them. In social terms, that is their tragedy, because it destroys them.

Postscript

Although perhaps best remembered for its torrid, much-parodied beach scene and its reconstruction of Pearl Harbor, *From Here to Eternity*, for Fred Zinnemann, was basically the story of the spirit of a soldier named Prewitt, as definitively acted by Montgomery Clift. The film swept the board for Oscars in 1954, but it was a disappointment for actor and director that Clift was not among the winners. (William Holden won the Best Actor Award for his performance in *Stalag 17*. The theory is that, as both Clift and Burt Lancaster were nominated for *From Here to Eternity*, it might have split the Academy vote.) As consolation, Fred's wife Renée sent Clift a miniature gold trumpet mounted like an Oscar. He treasured it for the rest of his life.

When Clift died in 1966, Zinnemann wrote the following tribute to him, published in *Sight and Sound* (Autumn 1966): "How well Monty Clift seemed to me when we last saw him, here in London, only a few short weeks ago. How enthusiastic he was about the next picture he was going to make—how alive and interested and excited by the new young English playwrights and actors. How certain he was that all his problems and difficulties had been surmounted and that the future looked bright once more. How can one describe the stature of the artist or the measure of the man—his relish and enjoyment of life, the fullness of his compassion, his stunning talent and his incredible sensibility? The best way is, perhaps, to tell you about two incidents that happened during the twenty years of our friendship. Between them, both these anecdotes seem to come close to Monty's essence and his spirit. When we made *The Search* together, Monty was very young. He had a distinguished stage career behind him, but was unknown to the cinema public. His first film, *Red River*, had not yet been released. In *The Search*, Monty played a young American soldier, the friend of a war orphan who had escaped form a displaced persons' camp. At the end of the showing, someone from the audience came to me and asked the question: 'Where did you find a *soldier* who could act so well?' The second incident happened several years later. By that time, Monty was already well-known. He and I had met in Venice and we went to dinner at La Fenice. I introduced him to the head waiter, whom I knew, and I said 'This is Montgomery Clift.' The head waiter took one look at Monty, said spontaneously 'You're an artist' and promptly burst into tears. Thereupon Monty also burst into tears and these two strangers hugged each other, sobbing away. How many artists will inspire that sort of love and emotion?"

The Nun's Story *(1959)*

> How could you train yourself to a detachment so deep-reaching that it cut you off from the very breath and heartbeat of your common humanity? She would never achieve that goal, she told herself with despair, unaware that when she had stifled her nurse's impulse to rush forward and give aid, she had already struggled up the first rise of that alpine climb.
> Later on, when she had trained herself to the exquisite charity of not seeming to see a sister in torment, kneeling alone in the chapel and crying quietly into her hands, or one who fasted furtively to starve an ardent nature into obedience, she would know that few of them

Three—Character Is Destiny

ever really reached the icy peaks of total detachment but only seemed to have done so, a position, in actual fact, much more perilous to maintain.
—Kathryn Hulme, *The Nun's Story*

"Who wants to see a documentary about how to become a nun?" This was the response of one motion picture executive when *The Nun's Story* was first proposed. But Zinnemann had read the galleys of the book and been absolutely gripped by the story it told. "It seemed to open the door to a new world," he said, anticipating the imagery of opening and closing doors which was to be one of the film's main visual features.

For Zinnemann, it was a project that offered the opportunity for thorough research into a community that had always challenged his imagination. The unknown quality of a nun's life appealed to the curiosity of Zinnemann the documentarian. The book also had an abundance of mountaineering imagery and a feeling for the gathering clouds of war that he might have absorbed almost subconsciously as something with which he could feel a personal involvement. Above all, it had the theme of individual conscience with which his films are preoccupied. In the book, it is defined thus: "And conscience, she thought, that intuitive sense of moral right and wrong which everyone is born with but which our Rule has trained and toughened with the twice daily exercise of it until it has grown from a still small voice to a functioning vital organ within us." That is absolutely what conscience means to a Fred Zinnemann protagonist: It is not a "still, small voice," it is a "functioning vital organ." And the irony of that passage in the book is that the nun's conscience becomes so highly developed that it leads her inexorably to leave the Rule. After 17 years in the Order, she discovers that she does not have the vocation. She may be able to deceive her sisters, but she cannot cheat God—or herself.

Setting up the film was not easy. Nevertheless, Zinnemann's "tenacity" (Joe Mankiewicz's word for that fierceness of will on which everyone remarked about Zinnemann's character) was not easily denied. Warners were persuaded that this could be an interesting film after Audrey Hepburn joined the cast. To make the film truly convincing, Zinnemann knew that he would need the cooperation of the Church. However, as with the negotiations with the

American Army on *From Here to Eternity*, how do you obtain cooperation from an institution for a film that could be regarded as critical of that institution? It can only be done by persuasive argument and by convincing the relevant people of your sincerity. Zinnemann and writer Robert Anderson had a number of meetings with highly placed members of the Church in Belgium, where the main story takes place, and there was considerable discussion on every possible aspect of the film and the script before it was passed. For example, there was a scene between the Mother Superior (Edith Evans) and the postulants, in which the former describes the nun's life as "a life against nature." It is a line that appears in the book, but it was a line that the religious adviser on the picture, Father Leo Lunders, queried. "We spent a whole afternoon debating that line," Zinneman recalled. "A suggested alternative was that it was a "life *above* nature," but I argued that it seemed to imply that, by donning the nun's habit, they had automatically achieved serenity and that, of course, was far from the truth. After a few days, a Jesuit friend, Father Harold Gardiner, suggested that the line should read: "*In a way* it is a life against nature," and to my surprise, this compromise was acceptable."

The nun's irrevocable decision to leave the convent, but only in proper accordance with Canon Law, must have required extraordinary toughness of spirit. The casting of the charming and attractive Audrey Hepburn in the role might seem to run counter to this toughness, but the danger of the film's sentimentalizing her struggle is avoided. This is partly because of Miss Hepburn's splendid performance, arguably her finest piece of character acting on film and a performance that is physically taxing and extremely attentive to detail. Its conviction is also due to the very skillful use the film makes of Hepburn's screen persona and the way this is related to the character of Sister Luke. She has often played a romantic in an alien world. (Her barely suppressed, inappropriate enthusiasm in the early part of the film for the majesty of religious ritual—what the book calls the "reverent wonder of her first impression"—is particularly well caught.) As in several of her films (*Roman Holiday*, *Sabrina* and later *Robin and Marian*), the cutting of her hair marks a significant change of identity. Even Sister Luke's close relationship with her father corresponds to the close relationship a Hepburn character on film has had with "father figures" (her screen romances with Hollywood's most eminent senior citizens such as Humphrey Bogart, Henry Fonda, Gary Cooper, Cary Grant, and Rex Harrison). This is not to say that *The Nun's Story* calculatedly used such Hepburn associations; it is simply to suggest the soundness of Zinnemann's casting instincts and to explain why it worked so well.

The other aspect of the casting, on which Zinnemann insisted, was that no major roles in the film should be played by Catholics. His insistence on this point basically reflected a desire to sustain the film's objectivity, so that the audience would be left free to make up its own mind. There would be no special pleading within the film for one side or the other.

This insistence on objectivity ultimately led to a disagreement between Zinnemann and the composer, Franz Waxman. Zinnemann felt that Waxman was allowing his anti–Catholic feelings to color his music too much, making some of the music for the church scenes sound as if they were written for dungeon scenes. Regarded by some as one of the finest examples of film music ever written, Waxman's score, researched and written in Rome, has many extraordinary things in it. There are the unnerving Schoenbergian flourishes to convey the tension and unease of the asylum scenes. An evocative drumbeat over the later convent sequences, after Sister Luke has returned from the Congo, skillfully suggests that the nun's own heartbeat is as yet more attuned to the rhythm of the life she has left than to the one to which she has returned. Above all, in the section towards the end of the film when Sister Luke prepares to divest herself of her nun's robes and don the clothes of her former life as Gabrielle, Waxman's hushed, Brucknerian string sound seems to hang in the air as a tension deeper than silence. But Waxman and Zinnemann had a major dispute over the music for the very end of the film. Waxman had written an exultant theme: Zinnemann wanted no music there at all. After the preview, the matter was discussed with Jack Warner who was siding with Waxman. "Warner said to me: 'Why don't you want music at the end?' and I answered, 'Why do you want music?' Warner said 'Because every Warner Brothers picture has music at the end.' That's when I had him. I said: 'If you have triumphant music at the end, that means that Warner Brothers are happy that the nun has left the convent. If you have downbeat music, you say that Warner Brothers regret and are sad that she went. Do you really want to take sides?' Even Warner backed away from that." There is little doubt that the profound silence in which the film ends is part of its meaning, its resonance and its courage. It is a more open conclusion than that of the book, the film's boldest stroke, and Zinnemann's finest "dying fall" ending, leaving the film hauntingly poised between serenity and defeat.

Once cast, the major actresses were each placed separately in convents around Paris so that they could witness details of the daily life in a religious community and absorb them for use in their performances. "I used to do the rounds at about ten o'clock in the morning—the nuns had been up about six hours by then—and check on how they were doing. This was in January 1958 and in the morning Audrey and the other actresses were absolutely blue with cold." The truthfulness of the performances owes much to this preparation. "In the Congo, some of the Africans were puzzled to see Peggy Ashcroft, who is a dedicated agnostic, sitting cross-legged and puffing on a small cigar or the others carrying makeup cases, because they were completely convinced from their performances that these were actual nuns. We explained to them that these were *American* nuns and that seemed to satisfy them." Dame Edith Evans told Zinnemann that she had got the clue she sought for her part in one sentence of the book, describing her character's posture: "The Reverend Mother Emmanuel's back never touched the back of a chair, no matter how weary she might be." For certain scenes, to make convincing the exacting physical requirements of a nun's life, Zinnemann used ballerinas from the Opera Theatre of Rome to perform the gestures of supplication of the nuns in the convent and chapel.

Also to enhance realism, he used a minimum of makeup and asked the actresses not to wear rouge or lipstick during the time of shooting the convent scenes in Italy, only to find that some of them drank wine during the lunch hour and returned with ruddy faces! (His usual makeup man, George Frost, commented interestingly to me on Zinnemann's close attention to this kind of detail: "We both strive for realism in make-up and he watched very closely for things like extras wishing to wear modern day makeup out of period with the film. When a pale look was required, he would get cross if he finds the people sun-bathing!")

The film was shot on location in what was then Stanleyville in the Belgian Congo and in Belgium itself, with the studio work being done in Rome. Originally, Zinnemann was enthusiastic about shooting the convent scenes in black and white and using color for the scenes in the Congo. He was finally persuaded to reject the idea, on the grounds that the return to black and white for the final part of the film might seem too much of a self-conscious device. Such is the restraint and austerity of Franz Planer's photography that the scenes in the convent *seem* to be shot in black and white anyway. The photographic contrast between convent and Congo seems to polarize the temperature of the experience between the two extremes of cold and heat, further intensifying the pressure on Sister Luke as she is pulled between the austerity of the mother house and the explosive fertility of the tropical mission. This contrast in physical climate mirrors the extreme inner tension of a character who feels herself being pulled between bells and drums, detachment and self-assertion, being Gabrielle the nurse or Sister Luke the nun.

In a way, *The Nun's Story* would seem to be an atypical Zinnemann subject. His most characteristic films are about an insistence on the individual self, yet the life of the nun is devoted to the "overcoming of self." In a sense, we have here the story of a person who discovers in time that she is not capable of that total detachment and absolute obedience. This tension between awareness or denial of self is absorbingly dramatized in *The Nun's Story*. It is reflected often in the contrast between the older, professed nuns and the novices: the former serene, rather blank; the latter often anxious, rather tense. Sometimes looks are exchanged which seem to imply a fleeting reciprocal envy: of calmness on the one hand, of vitality on the other. This tension is perhaps exemplified best in a single gesture: the pleasure of Sister Margharita (Mildred Dunnock) at seeing the return of Sister Luke from the Congo, an expression of personal pleasure she must instantly suppress.

When Gabrielle has first gone into the convent, Sister Margharita has said of her to Gabrielle's father: "Real spirit, I think." He has responded: "We call it stubbornness. You may too after a few weeks." Like the Marshal in *High Noon*, Prewitt in *From Here to Eternity* and More in *A Man for All Seasons*, she has to face up to the full consequences of her individual will. The ambiguities of pride have rarely been more subtly photographed in a film than in that scene where Sister Luke is asked to fail her medical exams to show humility. ("Courage needs witnesses," she says: In Fred Zinnemann's films, his characters, without exception, have to commit their most courageous acts alone.) Pride is an aspect of her self-respect, her courage, but it is also a dimension of her residual vanity, her ferocious will, and it is ultimately connected with her final feeling of failure. Even when she passes her exams triumphantly (fourth in a class of 80) inwardly she fails. It has been a triumph of knowledge but a failure of obedience—a triumph, like that of all the major characters in Zinnemann, "with hooks." The clinging to a sense of identity is fraught with pain and is often bought at a terrible cost. It means that the character is constantly under pressure. The time-span of the action of *High Noon* is about an hour and a half, and the time-span of *The Nun's Story* is 17 years, and yet, oddly enough, the films have the same relentlessness, the same sense of a main character who can hardly ever relax. It is one of the cleverest aspects of Robert Anderson's screenplay. Although we know that there are family developments around Sister Luke, although there is the onset of war, we see nothing of this. The film boldly keeps its concentration on the nun's life, keeps its camera on her face, in so doing, permitting the audience, as well as the character, no respite from her inner struggle.

Everything seems to intensify the pressure: her own unyielding character ("You must learn to bend a little or you'll break," she is told; and "With you, it's all or nothing"); her searing self-criticism (recalled by the Father's comment to Sister Luke in the confessional, "You're so *hard* on yourself, my child"). What is deemed to be good for her is sometimes tinged with disappointment. Every success is tainted with a sense of failure: Her passionate desire to be a good nurse to the natives leads into constant conflict with her professed vow to be, first of all, a nun. Her character is constantly driven by this duality and her instinctive compassion often rebounds on her with dreadful force. This is most fiercely dramatized in her fight with the dangerous lunatic, the "Archangel Gabriel" in the asylum when she has brought her water, despite being warned not to attend to her unaccompanied. The confrontation is terrifying because it is a nightmarish extension of her struggle with herself. (Even the woman's nickname, the "Archangel Gabriel" is tantalizing close to Sister Luke's real name, Gabrielle.) The madwoman's fierceness of will, religious dementia, rebellion against imprisonment within a cell, all find a horrific echo within Sister Luke herself as she struggles to prevent this fiend tearing off her nun's habit to reveal the secular self beneath.

It is a violent scene, and one matched in ferocity later when one of the Africans brutally murders a Sister in the Congo hospital (the splash of red blood on the white habit—in a film notable for its subdued photography—is a startling visual shock). It is strange that these moments seem more brutal than anything else in Fred Zinnemann's work—in *From Here to Eternity* or even in *The Day of the Jackal*. It is as if he were determined not to sentimentalize the life of the nuns. Their world is dramatized with remarkable dignity and is never seen simply as a retreat. It is a difficult life, which is too much for some. But there are no spiteful, vicious nuns; there are no sexual hysterics, as in a film like Powell and Pressburger's *Black Narcissus* (1947). They display enormous discipline in the face of war, sickness, violence: their cool, orderly strength is sometimes to be envied in comparison with the vibrant but often vicious outside world. The tempo of their lives—walking as if not in a hurry, but not loitering—produce a matching style from Fred Zinnemann that is unhurried, economical, entirely without frills. One might call *The Nun's Story* his most Dreyeresque film, the work of his which most powerfully recalls his intense admiration, as a young man, for *The Passion of Joan of Arc*.

Nevertheless, for Sister Luke, the life of a nun *is* "a life against nature." She gives this away in that moment when she is leaving the Congo and cries at that exotic bird, the royal crane: "I'm coming back, you beautiful thing. Coming back, do you hear?" For her, life is expressed in a defiant affirmation of nature. There is also the beautifully unstated feeling between her and Dr. Fortunati (vibrantly played by Peter Finch). The feeling between them, conveyed through looks and a mutual professional respect, is never defined nor discussed between them and the depth of it is never revealed except in one word by the nun. She has returned to the convent and, on seeing her, her father says she must have had a good doctor to have survived tuberculosis in the Congo. There is the tiniest pause before she replies, with a slightly self-conscious emphasis: "Exceptional." In a performance of remarkable physical and vocal control, Audrey Hepburn's inflection of this moment is supreme.

She is equally fine in the scene when Sister Luke hears the news of her father's death. The war has been the breaking point for her. It too is a violation of nature, its brutal progress represented entirely by nature imagery—individual shots of gaunt, twisted trees. Passivity—obedience without question—is not enough to combat such an evil. Nazism is something that it is not possible to forgive. When she learns of the murder of her father by the Germans, she paces the room, her inner struggle now externalized by the tense gesture of folding and crumpling the fatal telegram. She seems to hear the voices of the native boy Illunga (Errol John) when he expressed amazement at the nuns' pacific response to the murder of the Sister in the Congo hospital, and she realizes that his preference for revenge is rising in her heart. Her breakdown is finally signalled by her cry, "O Father ... Father...," a heart-rending cry that is filial, not spiritual. At the close of the scene, she is facing a black curtain and a quick fade to black seems to suck the nun ineluctably into a huge well of darkness that is her uncertain future.

A moving final meeting with the Reverend Mother (on a rain-soaked day that recalls the forlorn return of Sister Luke to the convent from the Congo) ends on a brief tracking shot which sees Sister Luke seated alone, vulnerable yet set on her course. The leave-taking scenes have a chill felt all the more powerfully because of the contrasting ceremonial welcome so many years before. As Gabrielle, she presses a bell and the door opens automatically: a suggestion perhaps of uncleanliness, of impersonal rejection, but also of the door's being *willed* open by her. Like all the great Fred Zinnemann films, *The Nun's Story* has had a tremendous sense of *journey*, transporting an audience into an unfamiliar physical and spiritual world and taking a character through an exhausting variety of experience

Lisa (Diana Lambert, left) passes a secret message to Sister Luke (Audrey Hepburn) which contains news of the murder of her father by the Nazis. From *The Nun's Story*, Warner Bros., 1959.

that, because of the nature of the character, culminates in a single individual destination along a lonely road. For the last shot, the camera stays inside the room as Gabrielle walks down a long road away from the convent, the open door causing her nun's robes to blow slightly in the wind, like ghosts. At the end of the road, she hesitates, wondering which way to turn, and then she turns right and is lost from view as the convent bells of obedience chime forlornly, as if vainly calling her back.

A Man for All Seasons *(1966)*

> Thomas More, as I wrote him, became for me a man with an adamantine sense of his own self. He knew where he began and left off, what area of himself he

could yield to the encroachment of his enemies, and what to the encroachments of those he loved. It was a substantial area in both cases for he had a proper sense of fear and was a busy lover. Since he was a clever man and a great lawyer he was able to retire from those areas in wonderfully good order, but at length he was asked to retreat from that final area where he located his self. And there this supple, humorous, unassuming and sophisticated person set like metal, was overtaken by an absolutely primitive rigour, and could no more be budged than a cliff.
—Robert Bolt, Preface, *A Man for All Seasons*

MORE: But what matters to me is not whether it's true or not, but that I believe it to be true, or rather not that I *believe* it, but that *I* believe it.... I trust I make myself obscure?
—*A Man for All Seasons*, Act II

The film director's job in bringing a successful stage play to the screen can sometimes seem little more than "window dressing," filigree patterns around basic material that has already proved its worth. Fred Zinnemann's work on *A Man for All Seasons* is something more than that, although he would be the first to attribute the film's success to the quality of Robert Bolt's original play and the skill with which Bolt adapted it to the requirements of the screen. His main task as a director, as he saw it, was to find a style that would preserve the integrity of the material and to assemble a cast whose strength and quality in depth would clearly surpass anything that was possible in most theater companies.

Nevertheless, at the time, it must have seemed a riskier venture than it appears in retrospect. With the exception of Peter Glenville's successful film, *Becket* (1964), there was not much evidence then of a vogue for costume drama. Hollywood was discovering permissiveness and loosening the codes governing the control of sex and violence on the screen; Britain was still swinging cinematically with alternately vivacious and sour pictures of contemporary society, as in Richard Lester's *The Knack* and John Schlesinger's *Darling*. Also, Zinnemann's previous screen adaptations of stage successes (*The Member of the Wedding*, *Oklahoma!*, *A Hatful of Rain*) had not proved commercially very successful, and he was working in a genre in which he had not worked before. Uppermost in his mind, and that of Columbia Pictures, must have been the thought that it was his first film since the strangely disappointing *Behold a Pale Horse*. It was a feature of Zinnemann's career, however, that his new film would always be quite different from the one before. He also often had the priceless knack of following one of his major financial failures with one of his biggest commercial successes—*High Noon* after *Teresa*, *From Here to Eternity* after *The Member of the Wedding*, *The Nun's Story* after *A Hatful of Rain*. There were two particular lessons he learned from the failure of *Behold a Pale Horse* that he put into immediate effect on this new film: not to assume that the audience knew anything about the historical context in which the story was set; and not to make any compromises on casting.

The role of Sir Thomas More was perhaps one of the most coveted of screen roles of the time (Charlton Heston's *Journals* record how desperately he would have liked it). Considering the unfashionable nature of the piece, there must have been considerable pressure to insure against possible failure by putting a bankable star in the lead. But Zinnemann never wavered in his conviction that Paul Scofield should play the role. Scofield had triumphed on the stage with it; the role was ingrained. "He needed very little direction, other than early guidance in gauging his performance to the requirements of the camera, and a reminder that acting on the screen is the art of *re*-acting." Once he had assimilated that, Scofield was supreme.

The other casting was carefully considered. Zinnemann knew that Wendy Hiller would give the ostensibly simple character of More's wife, Alice, a vibrancy and leonine strength and anger that is particularly important for the full poignancy of the prison scene when More has to say farewell to the family. Susannah York would have absolutely the right independence of spirit for More's beloved daughter, Margaret; Leo McKern, who had played the Common Man in the stage production, could revel in the devious and dangerous intellect of Thomas Cromwell; Robert Shaw could be an unexpectedly youthful, sunny but capricious and dangerous Henry VIII ("*not* the Holbein Henry," as Bolt insisted in his notes to the play). For the key role of the weak and treacherous Richard Rich,

Zinnemann cast John Hurt, who had made only one insignificant film appearance before *A Man for All Seasons* and whom he had seen on stage in David Halliwell's *Little Malcolm and His Struggle Against the Eunuchs*. Hurt's performance was to be a powerful indication of his future prowess as a film actor.

Perhaps the most unusual piece of casting is that of Orson Welles as Cardinal Wolsey. The scene between More and Wolsey is one of the most effective in the film. In an interview in Ivan Butler's *The Making of Feature Films: A Guide* (Pelican 1971), the designer John Box mentioned that, in reality, Wolsey's room would have been much bigger, but he and Zinnemann agreed that dramatically what they wanted was a sense of claustrophobia, a feeling that there is no air in the room. The power of the scene comes from this sense of being under intense pressure ("pressure" is a key word in the film), and from a sense of confinement that prefigures More's ultimate imprisonment, his world of influence finally narrowed down to himself and to the slit in the wall of his cell. The intensity of the scene is reinforced by the oppressive use of red, that seems to threaten the prospect of blood-letting to come, and by the sheer scale of Welles' presence that makes Wolsey seem a solid mass of brooding intimidation.

Although Zinnemann was typically attentive to period detail (he was not pleased to find on one occasion that the lawn on one location had been clearly cut by modern machinery), he was sympathetic to imaginative licence if it seemed to enhance the drama of a scene. For Henry VIII's boat trip to More's house, John Box said that, in reality, the vessels would probably have been much larger but that he and Fred wanted something that would instantly convey the nature of the occasion: that it was a light-hearted excursion more than a formal visit. Part of the tension of the subsequent argument between the King and More comes from this sense of a picnic that has gone wrong, of an occasion in which the courtesies of informality have been breached. A casual country visit abruptly seems a matter of life and death (when the King menacingly switches conversational tack with the words, "Touching this other business mark you, I'll have no opposition...," even the wind starts up). Suddenly there is the indecorous spectacle of the host being harangued by his guest.

In terms of the adaptation, the main discussion between the director and Robert Bolt concerned the character of the Common Man, a kind of "bastardized Brechtian device," as Bolt called him, who on stage had linked the events and inhabited a variety of roles (steward, boatman, jailer, executioner) as he followed More's inexorable descent. He was the composite pragmatic man: a self-serving survivor in a slippery world. Bolt thought he was too theatrical a device to work on the screen. But Zinnemann wanted, if possible, to keep him. They worked very hard for two months thinking of ways to handle the problem, but eventually he had to agree with Bolt that it probably would not work, and the parts in the film are played by individual actors. "But I was sorry to lose that character: I liked the idea of someone who would do anything just to keep breathing...."

For Robert Bolt, Sir Thomas More was "a hero of selfhood." More thought of himself in the First Person, belying the tendency (which Bolt saw as common to the modern day) to think of himself in the Third Person as an instrument of society or in the classification imposed on him by society. For this reason, he cannot accede to the social or political pressure of others, even if (as it often does in a Zinnemann film) it might lead to physical torture. He cannot take an oath pledging himself to a lie, because, as More says, "when a man takes an oath, he's holding his own self in his own hands. Like water. And if he opens his fingers *then*—he needn't hope to find himself again." More has all the requisites of the Zinnemann protagonist, a man prepared and ultimately required to sacrifice everything on a point of principle. As Bolt wrote, and it is true for all of these Zinnemann heroes, the issue is basically a simple one for his hero and he never has any doubts over what he must do: What is difficult is the outcome. Everything in *A Man for All Seasons* gathers to a single superb image—the forward tracking shot as More walks into the courtroom alone, faced by his accusers and by interested spectators. He advances through an increasingly narrow entrance, which not only signifies the inhibitions of his freedom consequent upon his moral decision, but the straight narrow path which has been his route through the film: the only one he can follow. ("For that moment I had always the image in my mind of a bull coming into the ring, as seen from the bull's point of view.")

The play has sometimes been criticized for idealizing More too much, not only making him indubitably in the right (if that is so, of course, it makes his fate all the harder to bear), but giving him all the witty lines as well. Although he is clearly a hero to Bolt and Zinnemann, the film does bring out those elements of the material that do suggest a more rounded view of the man. Scofield's impeccably dry, donnish performance keeps the flaws as well as the greatness of the man in view. Bolt had anticipated more recent historical research (for example, Jaspar Ridley's 1982 book, *The Statesman and the Fanatic: Thomas Wolsey and Thomas More*) which were to stress More's political opportunism and his cruelty to his wife. In film and play, More seems rather calculatedly obsequious to the King, and only belatedly taking cognizance of what his stand might mean to his family; his imperious call to his wife, "Woman, mind your house!" is met by her vehement response, "I *am* minding my house." More does flaunt the role of patriarch in his own house; is frequently patronizing when dealing with people of lower intellect; and is politically naïve. Certain pronouncements, said in a tone of lofty finality, are sometimes to rebound ironically against him (for example: "When they see I'm silent, they'll want nothing better than to leave me silent"). All of this is not to deny the stature of More's character, it is to suggest that the character is presented with rather more of the stuff of humanity than he is often credited for. Goodness, after all, is a very difficult thing to dramatize.

There is a nice moment in the film (not in the play) when More is travelling home by boat after his meeting with Wolsey, and inspecting a goblet he has been given by a woman whose case comes up in the Court of Requests. It is a bribe, he knows, and he throws it into the water. Interestingly, what he does not do is offer it to his boatman, who could presumably use the money from selling it. It is conscience without consideration. In fact, the boatman quickly fishes it out and the goblet, with all its tainted associations, is appropriately to wind up with Rich. More might wish to renounce the corruption of the world with idealistic gestures, but it will re-surface and attempt to submerge him again sooner or later.

It is clear why the character of More—a Tudor prisoner of conscience—would appeal to Zinnemann. But what would equally attract him about the play is the portrayal of community and political atmosphere. Thematically the play is less about Catholicism than a kind of McCarthyism. One of the striking things about the film is its atmosphere of spying and paranoia, of interrogation and the taking of oaths. People are constantly looking over their shoulders (More in his scene with Wolsey, Rich in the tavern with Cromwell). Simply to toss a stone into the darkness is to reveal someone lurking behind a tree. Norfolk can have what he believes to be a private conversation with More and have one of his statements from that occasion ("This is England, not Spain") quoted back at him later by a gloating Cromwell. The film is about people who are afraid to talk, or people who are dangerous to know. It is a society of potential informers. Even a line like More's "You threaten like a dockside bully" brings the ostensibly incongruous but actually relevant specter of *On the Waterfront* into this situation. In his defence, More is effectively pleading the Fifth Amendment. The impact of McCarthyism undoubtedly provided Zinnemann with a valuable frame of reference for this film. It gives a modern pertinency to some of Norfolk's exchanges with More: "You lay traps for me!"/I show you the times."

A Man for All Seasons is a political film: it contrasts people who see life in terms of power and privilege and those who see it in terms of pride and principle. The film begins and ends with symbols of power (the "King's Beasts" of Hampton Court, the Cardinal's seal) and this is continued throughout, particularly in the visual concentration on the chain of the Chancellor's office, which is ultimately to weigh on Sir Thomas so heavily that he cannot remove it without the aid of his daughter. The film is about such symbols of office and what people are prepared to do to get them.

In the scene of the King's visit to More, Zinnemann has made considerable use of a patch of mud on the shore, in which the King has trodden when he has disembarked. (Its inspiration is the early line of Wolsey to More when he sees the King from his window: "He's been to play in the muck again: he's been with Anne Boleyn"). More scrupulously keeps clear, but Rich falls right in it, an indication of how he is to be besmirched by his association with Cromwell (Cromwell's question on this occasion, "Are you coming my way, Rich?," refers to more than just a journey) and is to

The King (Robert Shaw) arrives with his entourage for a fateful visit to Sir Thomas More in *A Man for All Seasons*, Columbia Pictures, 1966. "I researched the paintings of Holbein for this film as a way of trying to get to the human being behind the costume," said Zinnemann.

become one of the King's men. A clever establishing shot of the church reflected upside-down in a stream cues in the wedding of Henry and Anne (Vanessa Redgrave) and demonstrates how the Church's values have somersaulted to accommodate the wishes of the King. From this point forward, More's moral ascendancy is visually matched to his physical decline, and the other way round in the case of Rich, whose increasing corruption is signalled by his ever more extravagant finery.

These two images confront each other finally in the courtroom, More stooped but spiritually ascendant, Rich lavishly attired but, in the terms of the drama, irredeemably damned. Significantly, More draws attention to Rich's chain of office, which is essentially the price paid for collusion towards More's execution. "Why, Richard, it profits a man nothing to give his soul for the whole world.... But for Wales!" Performance and direction are finely judged throughout this scene. Simply by the posture he adopts, Scofield is able to convey the impression in the trial that More is judging his accusers, rather than the other way round. By keeping the camera at a distance, often at moments of great passion, Zinnemann can give proper weight to More's rhetoric; give the sense of him in the final moments as an actor in the theater playing commandingly to the gallery; and give the cinema audience the equivalent viewpoint of the trial spectator, watching from the wings. The final bleak narration, strikingly similar to the strategy Costa-Gavras was to use to underline the political cynicism of the film *Z*, suggests that More's sacrifice was individually heroic but politically inconsequential. The continuing political intrigues mentioned, leading to Cromwell's execution and the elevation of Rich to More's former position as Chancellor, are an ironic comment on the efficacy of Government and of Justice. But loyalty to his conscience was more important to Sir Thomas than loyalty to the State.

In some respects, More is different from other leading Zinnemann protagonists considered in the chapter. He is not naturally an outsider, being initially perfectly at home in his world. Also, unlike the others, who are silent or taciturn and often cannot put into words the profundity of their feelings, More is extremely articulate. Although he cannot explain to his family the reasons for his behavior, for fear of involving them in his "treason" he can put into words that sense of self which is so important to these Zinnemann characters. In a way he speaks for Marshal Kane, Prewitt and Sister Luke. With regard to what Wolsey calls More's "moral squint," he is absolutely in their mold. His shield is his wit and the Law. This line of defense breaks down over the issue of a Loyalty Oath pledging endorsement of the King's marriage. His conversation with Margaret about this Bill takes place in a howling gale, a fulfilment of More's earlier prophecy of the wind that would sweep the country if the Rule of Law were abused or ignored. Unlike Richard Rich, who is "a feather for each wind that blows," but like Sister Luke in *The Nun's Story*, More will not bend with the wind. It breaks his body finally—but not his spirit, his self.

CHAPTER FOUR

Variations on a Theme

The Member of the Wedding *(1953)*

> "I think I have a vague idea what you were driving at," she said. "We all of us somehow caught. We born this way or that way and we don't know why. But we caught anyhow. I born Berenice. You born Frankie. John Henry born John Henry. And maybe we wants to widen and bust free. But no matter what we do we still caught."
> —Carson McCullers, *The Member of the Wedding*

> It was better to be in a jail where you could bang the walls than in a jail you could not see.
> —*The Member of the Wedding*

The Member of the Wedding was Fred Zinnemann's last film for Stanley Kramer, made after *High Noon* (which had not at that time been released) and before *From Here to Eternity*, whose success was to give a massive fillip to Zinnemann's career. It is a deeply felt film that shows enormous sympathy for Carson McCullers' characterization and a real feeling for the humor as well as the pathos of the material. Nevertheless, it did dismal business at the box office, a disappointing fate for those who had put so much heart into its making. Talking of the thin line between success and failure in the film industry, Zinnemann often quoted Sean O'Casey's dictum: "The theater is no place for those who bleed easily."

Several factors probably contributed to the film's commercial failure. For budgetary reasons and also because of difficulties in fashioning a satisfactory script, it had been decided to adapt the film not from the original novel but from the stage play derived from it, which in turn prompted a decision to shoot the film mainly in the studio. This sense of confinement would not have helped the film's prospects at a time when wide-screen and spectacle were being offered as the most viable alternative to television. In transplanting the work from stage to screen, Zinnemann and Kramer also decided to transplant the original cast. In one sense, this was an entirely happy decision: Julie Harris, Ethel Waters and Brandon De Wilde all knew their parts intimately, and one cannot imagine their being played better. But at that time, a film without stars was a dubious box office prospect, and both Miss Harris and Brandon De Wilde were making their screen debuts. The posters talked excitedly of Julie Harris' "sensational screen debut," but Miss Harris' contribution does not deliver that kind of star promise: It is instead a brilliant piece of character acting. Also the advertising's lurid gloss on the heroine's passage from innocence to experience gives a false promise of sexual sensation (a premonition of *Baby Doll?*) that belies the film's sensitivity to the heroine and cannot have endeared it to gullible customers. Above all, *The Member of the Wedding*, like *The Sundowners* and *Five Days One Summer*, is one of those Zinnemann films that deals not so much with a plot but with a *mood*: always a brave and fascinating film to make, and always tricky in a narrative-orientated cinema.

For Zinnemann, the theatrical origins of the material presented different problems, or challenges. The theatrical emphasis of the work would run contrary to his documentary roots, his preference for location shooting, his desire to get close to the "real" people. Also, as a rule, his preference, if possible, was to work from short stories or original ideas rather than from novels or plays. It permitted more space for the imagination and the opportunity to expand and develop the basic theme in your own way. Prior to this film, *The Search* and *High Noon* had been worked out like that; in the future, *Julia* and *Five Days One Summer* were to profit from that approach. But *The Member of the Wedding* was already well set. In this first film of his to be based on a stage play, Zinnemann had to devise a means of retaining the quality of the original without diluting it by "opening it out," but at the same time maintain the visual interest of the audience. He does this very successfully in three ways. Because he respected good writing, he is a director like Wyler or Mankiewicz with that unobtrusive art of filming dialogue which, through an adroit balance of shot, makes an audience attend to every word said. He uses occasional deep-focus to give each frame different layers of meaning and humour (for example, when Frankie is on the phone to the police about her missing "Persian" tomcat, Berenice is simultaneously visible in the background of the shot squirming and giggling at the tale she is overhearing—"He's no more Persian that I is!"). Finally, the theatricality of the piece and its challenge to his visual imagination means that the set is more richly detailed and expressive than is sometimes the case. "The empty, ugly house," about which Frankie moans, is an effective extension of what she feels about herself, a correlative to her inner disorder and her bursts of self-hatred (splinters get in her feet, a knife quivers in the door).

With the cast's coming straight from the stage to screen, a problem for the director was that, after two years of playing the roles, their performances were somewhat crystallized. In that regard, Zinnemann certainly had some difficulty with Ethel Waters: "If she had moved left on a particular line in the stage production and I asked her to move right, I was in for an argument. She used to say: "God is my director." I competed as best I could." Ultimately, none of these restrictions seems to matter too much. Ethel Waters is magnificent, the performance preserved with the sensitivity Zinnemann had shown years before in his treatment of the Negro on screen in *The Story of Dr. Carver*. As John Henry, Brandon De Wilde brings a delightful puckish humor that is a valuable counterpoint to Frankie's intensity. As Frankie, the self-lacerating 12-year-old misfit adrift in the vacuum between childhood and puberty, Julie Harris gives one of those performances that seems more lived than acted. The character's tension between defying the world and yet yearning to belong is rendered with unforgettable poignancy.

In talking to me, Harris remembered that her main fear in the

Frankie (Julie Harris) converses intently with John Henry (Brandon de Wilde) while Berenice (Ethel Waters) looks on in the background. From *The Member of the Wedding*, Columbia Pictures, 1953.

film was the danger of giving a performance that was too "big" for the screen; and therefore Zinnemann's main directing task was to assess and adjust the scale of her projection. It is calculated with some subtlety. All theatricality cannot be removed from the performance because Frankie is a theatrical person, given to self-dramatization. Her loudness has to be retained, because that is a dimension of her dilemma: No one really listens to her—her brother, her father, even at times Berenice. (The deafness of adults to the pain of children is to have a tragic outcome in the fate of poor John Henry, who is ignored by Berenice at precisely the time he most needs help.) If Harris' performance is big, the reason is that Frankie *is* big for her age, emphasizing her sense of freakishness and alienation; she *does* use words that are too big for her, relishing their sound without understanding their meaning; and above all, she is trying to grow up too fast. She ventures into the adult world before she (or the world) is ready. On the first occasion, she tries to climb into her brother's wedding car and is bodily pulled out. On the second, she leaves home and ventures into the town, and the adult world is vividly presented as a discordant and frightening confusion of sights and sounds—sinister dark alleys, overheard marital squabbles, threatening masculinity—leading to Frankie's flight (when no one is chasing her) from darkness into morning and back to the world she knows.

The film's sense of confinement may have harmed its commercial chances, but it seems highly appropriate to Frankie's sense of her own situation. She feels suffocated by her environment. She feels trapped inside her own character, wishing she were someone else, and constantly changing her name—Frankie, Frances, F. Jasmine—as if it will magically confer on her a different personality. In Harris' performance, Frankie is always picking at herself: admonishing, improving, restless, touchy; and everything about her appearance (her rough crew-cut, her grubby elbows) betokens her desperate confusion of identity. She is a tomboy but a tormented one, played wholly without cuteness or sentimentality. She longs to look feminine, but the image of elegance she presents is incongruous (like her choice of dress for the wedding whose inappropriateness for her is colorfully summarized by Berenice: "I ain't accustomed to seeing human Christmas trees in August"). Like a number of heroines in Zinnemann's films (like Teresa, Alma in *From Here to Eternity*, Laurey in *Oklahoma!*, Lillian in *Julia*, Kate in *Five Days One Summer*), Frankie is a dreamer, whose dreams turn into nightmares and who has to live through their consequences in order to come to terms with reality. Frankie's most intense dream is her fantasy of accompanying her brother and his wife after their wedding: "This coming Sunday when my brother and his bride leave this town, I'm going with the two of them to Winter Hill. And after that to whatever place they will ever go. I love the two of them so much and we belong together. I love the two of them so much because they are the *we* of me." She will not accompany them, of course, and her rejection will be a humiliating but important stage in her coming to terms with herself, in a way discovering the "me" of "we."

The "we of me" speech—one of the highlights of the film, radiantly shot and acted—has been triggered by Frankie's listening to the sound of Berenice's foster brother Honey (James Edwards) as he plays his horn. The solo has something of the feeling of Prewitt's "Taps" in *From Here to Eternity* which touches everyone. Music is very important in the film. Alex North's score ranges from the most sensitive accompaniment of privileged moments (such as Frankie's soliloquy, or Berenice's searing description of the night her first husband died) to dramatic intensification of passionate encounters (the harsh jazzy blues for Frankie's excursion into the adult world and her straying into the "Blue Moon" Hotel). There is also the hymn ("I sing because I'm happy, I sing because I'm free") which Frankie, Berenice and John Henry croon together in their moment of perfect communication; and that lovely moment when Berenice, after her monologue about her husband Ludie, hums in counterpoint as Frankie continues her thought. So much of the film is musically conceived (even the stumbling onto the awkward topic of sex is nervously accompanied by the discordant fumblings on the keyboard of a nearby piano tuner) that Honey's horn solo as the cue for Frankie's most heartfelt speech seems movingly appropriate.

Honey might seem a minor character but, thematically, he is important to the whole structure. Just as Frankie feels an unwanted stranger in her world, so does Honey in his. On the night when Frankie tries to escape from her world, so Honey tries to escape from his (after he has accidentally run over a white man in his car). Both Frankie and Honey have similar odd bouts of violent rage that Berenice has to control. Both of them feel excluded but whereas Frankie's struggles are with herself, Honey's are with the whole social structure. The outsider in American culture is the Negro.

This might be the reason that, at the end of the film, Zinnemann, with his sympathy for the outsider, chooses to stay with Berenice rather than with Frankie. Her heavy, motionless melancholy in that last scene, the result of her self-reproach for the death of John Henry, casts a doleful shadow across Frankie's newfound stability. Frankie's agonies have been transient growing pains, but adult pain lasts; "Your road is already strange to me now," Berenice tells Frankie, and the weight of her sadness (disclosed in her mannerism of humming to herself when her heart is breaking) dominates the final scene, setting Frankie's enthusiasm and adjustment against Berenice's isolation and emptiness.

Maybe the sadness of the ending did not help the film find an audience either. It is a little downbeat and unresolved for mainstream cinema. The worlds the film evokes—that of the teenager in turmoil, that of the underprivileged Negro—might seem strange and specialized, requiring an effort of empathy and imagination. Ironically, in defining why the film did not make money, one seems simultaneously to define why it is so refreshing, honest and good. "I'm not sure even today it would do any better," Julie Harris told me, "it was a small-scale film, an 'art' film. It was made by people who simply loved the material." It shows.

Oklahoma! *(1955)*

The critic David Thomson once remarked that, in this film, Fred Zinnemann had taken the exclamation mark out of *Oklahoma!* The reason is that the musical is a Utopian form in the imperative tense, delivering an exuberant message at the top of its voice: everything, in fact, that is the absolute reverse of what one expects from Zinnemann. His films make you think; musicals make you forget. It was precisely that escapist joyousness to which he had responded when he had seen *Oklahoma!* on the stage in the 1940s, but that would be difficult for him to reproduce on the screen.

Why, then, did he do the film? The simple answer, he said, was: "I was asked—by two good friends, Arthur Hornblow, Jr., and Mike Todd." (Arthur Hornblow Jr. had given Zinnemann one of his first opportunities in Hollywood as assistant to Busby Berkeley and the great cameraman Gregg Toland on *The Kid from Spain* in 1932. Mike Todd was one of the instigators of Cinerama—the word is his—and of Todd-AO, a boisterous, ebullient showman whom Zinnemann liked very much.) The novelty of making his first film in color would also have been an attraction. The technical challenge of Todd-AO, the process in which *Oklahoma!* was filmed but in which it has rarely been screened, was another temptation. For a European-born director, who had spent most of his life in America, such an American project might be a fascinating way to test his acclimatization. (Billy Wilder was to take up a similar challenge in a year's time with another quintessentially American subject, *The Spirit of St. Louis*.) Also, just as *From Here to Eternity* had been a triumphant success of "casting against type" for the actors, Zinnemann might have been drawn to the principle of casting himself against type in agreeing to make a musical. Why should it not work for directors as well as actors? Although he had not directed a musical before, he was musically knowledgeable. Also he had shown, in *High Noon*, a sensitivity to the background of the American West, and particularly that period where the pioneering spirit has to be domesticated and the wilderness must become civilization, that is relevant to the material of *Oklahoma!*

What would have happened if either Paul Newman or James Dean had played the role of Curly? They were two of the people considered, and were both at that time unknowns. Newman did not want his voice dubbed and wanted to sing the songs himself, which, understandably, did not match up to the musical requirements of either Rodgers or Hammerstein. The case of Dean was more interesting. He had been spotted on television by Zinnemann's wife, Renée, and invited to an audition for the role of Curly on the 35th floor of an exclusive hotel, the Pierre in New York. When he had not arrived 30 minutes after the appointed time, Zinnemann began to be concerned, only for Dean to appear finally in a state of some outrage and anger. He had come dressed for the part in worn jeans and cowboy boots and had been refused entry! He had finally to smuggle his way back into the building by coming up in the freight elevator. "His test was magnificent, easily the most impressive for that part, but the problem was the same as with Paul Newman: Rodgers and Hammerstein wanted a singer who could act, and Dean could not sing." Finally cast in the main roles were Gordon MacRae, who could sing magnificently and act a little, and Shirley Jones, who had originally been in the chorus of Rodgers and Hammerstein shows and who made a completely assured singing and acting screen debut. Also in the cast by this time was Rod Steiger as Jud, a man who could sing well enough and act phenomenally and whose scenes with MacRae were to rupture the stylistic unity of the film.

The film was shot in both Todd-AO and CinemaScope, because it was not known at the time how many theaters would be able to accommodate the new screen process. This in itself was an absorbing exercise, for Zinnemann rapidly found that the cast tried very hard for the new process but were rather more casual and relaxed when appearing before the CinemaScope camera. This often meant that their performances in the latter process came over as more natural and spontaneous. He found it advisable to switch the cameras around so that, as far as possible, the actors did not know in advance which camera was filming them.

It was a happy and enjoyable film to make. Ironically, most of the film was shot in Arizona because Oklahoma, by the time of the film, was too industrialized and had too many oil wells to disguise. The film was politely received by press and public, doing moderately well but somehow not having the same runaway success as other Rodgers and Hammerstein adaptations of that time, *The King and I* and *South Pacific* (and later, *The Sound of Music*). For this comparative failure, Zinnemann blamed no one but himself: "I didn't really know enough about what makes a musical go. I went for the realism in the human story which was valid enough, but the emphasis I gave to it unbalanced the film. Rod Steiger's performance as Jud is excellent, but I gave it too much weight. Jud is supposed to be a stage villain whose death everyone is meant to cheer. But because of Steiger's performance, Jud comes over as a deeply neurotic, complex personality, very much in need of help which is not forthcoming, and, when people cheer his death, they're made to look quite cruel, instead of being a warm-hearted, caring community. I ought to have spotted this break in style during the film, but I didn't."

There is no doubt that Steiger's performance dominates the film, and this has enormous consequences. The film's imagery is polarized between light and dark: between Curly's "O What a Beautiful Morning" and Jud's smokehouse; between Curly's white-clad girl and between Jud's dark ladies who adorn his wall. But because Jud's world is realized so intensely, much more than Curly's, the weight of sympathies is violently disrupted towards the "villain."

Agnes DeMille described *Oklahoma!* as a "pastoral opera," but, because of Rod Steiger's performance, the snake in this Edenic paradise assumes large and complex dimensions. The bit hit song of the show—Curly's and Laurey's duet "People Will Say We're in Love"—seems frivolous when set beside the ballet "Out of My Dreams," in which Jud appears as a nightmare projection of Laurey's subconscious desires. In the ballet, color and imagery suggest a demonic hell, virtue is defenseless (there is a mocking arrangement of "I'm Just a Girl Who Can't Say No") and a deflowered heroine reels in a terrifying world of devils and darkness, masks and corridors. Although the scene was choreographed brilliantly by Agnes DeMille, in dramatic terms it features a recognizable Zinnemann situation. It shows a romantic heroine dreaming about a situation which, in reality, might result in a rude, unpleasant shock. The fantasy turns into nightmare, full of foreboding. The problem with this, in the context of *Oklahoma!* is that, although it is interesting in the evolving career of Zinnemann, it is not so appropriate for a Utopian musical.

Also one should say that it is not only the dramatic quality of Rod Steiger's performance that throws the balance of the picture. There is no doubt that Jud is the character that would interest the director most. He is an outsider, someone who, to borrow a James Joyce phrase, is "excluded from life's feast" (compare Curly and Laurey's duet in the orchard, its sense of fecundity, with Jud's unsuccessful bid for Laurey's hamper at the dance, where the women are presented as dishes for the delectation of the men). If music be the food of love, it is significant that Jud is given no song of his own ("Poor Jud is Dead" is actually Curly's song—a characteristic sick joke—with which Jud harmonizes, because he is moved by this sad image of himself). Jud is starved of affection, of sexual companionship, the need for which has slowly been perverted into that expressive room of his imagination, with its lewd pictures and sleazy atmosphere. When he peers in at the window at Laurey and again at the wedding, one gets an unpleasant sense of him as voyeur but also a sense of his exclusion, a character tormented by his own unattractiveness. Laurey does lead him on, by choosing him out of pique to accompany her to the dance (rather like Bathsheba's rash valentine to Boldwood in Hardy's *Far from the Madding Crowd*, that is to have disastrous consequences).

Hands on hips, an angry Jud (Rod Steiger, right center) prepares to square up to Curly (Gordon MacRae, left center) while an anxious Laurey (Shirley Jones) looks on. From *Oklahoma!*, Twentieth Century–Fox, 1955.

What comes over from this portrayal of Jud is not so much one-dimensional evil as isolation and frustration. His buggy ride with Laurey has a real sense of obsession, Laurey a blonde wish-fulfilment beside him offering, temporarily, precariously, the possibility of a new life. Often superb at exposing the darker impulses of his heroes, Zinnemann is equally interesting here in the way he implies the flawed humanity and aspirations of his villain. Even at the end, when Jud sets fire to the barn in a manner that recalls the premonitory flames in Laurey's dream, it seems more an act of twisted love than demonic evil: If he cannot have Laurey, then no one else will. Beside Jud, Curly seems positively superficial.

Nothing in the film rivals the force of Jud. However, it has a pleasing lyricism in the outdoor sequences, and the occasional framing of man against nature recalls the directorial eye that gave us *The Wave* and anticipates the visual stylist of *The Sundowners* and *Five Days One Summer*. There are some deft images which offer a visualization of the lyrics (corn as high as an elephant's eye, the famous low-angle shot of the geese as they scurry away from the surrey with the fringe on top). The matching of style to song is often quite adroit. The idea behind "The Surrey with the Fringe on Top" is that it is a white lie, sung to impress the heroine (revealing Curly's propensity to brag and Laurey's to fantasize). Accordingly, the song ends with a shot of neatly judged comic deflation, the camera tracking to reveal a single horse. Even "People Will Say We're in Love" is a song that, at least partly, admonishes the heroine for being a tease, for denying the reality of her feelings. One can understand why the director felt "Out of My Dreams" had to be dramatized so forcefully: to explore the dark potential of Laurey's flirtatiousness, the sexual fear that might lurk at the root of her prim romanticism. However, it is a theme more suitable for D.H. Lawrence and Thomas Hardy than for Richard Rodgers and Oscar Hammerstein, and Zinnemann's inadvertent emphasis on such aspects eventually dilutes the musical's escapism. *High Noon* has been described as a Western for people who do not like Westerns. To some extent, *Oklahoma!* is a musical for people who do not like musicals. It does not have the genre's requisite bounce and joy, but it does have its moments of drama.

A Hatful of Rain *(1957)*

A Hatful of Rain seemed to have a lot of potential. It reunited Fred Zinnemann with producer Buddy Adler, with whom he had worked so successfully on *From Here to Eternity*. After the diversion of *Oklahoma!*, it looked a return to serious territory: a study of a man, tortured in the Korean War, who had become a drug addict. But the film on all levels was only a modest success. It seemed a pause in Zinnemann's career rather than a step forward, in some ways a review and reprise of former themes.

The play by Michael Vincent Gazzo, who is probably better known as an actor (notably for his Oscar-nominated performance as Frankie Pentangeli in *The Godfather: Part II*), had been a big success on Broadway. Zinnemann set about researching the background with his customary thoroughness, spending two months with the narcotics squad in New York and talking to dozens of addicts. The text was also fully rehearsed with the actors before they started shooting, an experience that Anthony Franciosa (who described Zinnemann to me as "an extraordinarily sensitive man, with a great deal of honesty about him") found an interesting and valuable departure from what he had heard of standard Hollywood film practice. Franciosa and Henry Silva (making his film debut as the sinister pusher "Mother") were two of the survivors from the original stage cast. The parts of husband and wife, played on Broadway by Ben Gazzara and Shelley Winters, were played in the film by Don Murray and Eva Marie Saint. Saint had made an auspicious Oscar-winning debut in Kazan's *On the Waterfront* (1954), and Don Murray had made a favorable impression playing opposite Marilyn Monroe in *Bus Stop* (1956). Apart from the experienced support of Lloyd Nolan as the father, it was a cast of relatively fresh faces, generally a good sign in a Zinnemann film.

The film's treatment of the subject of drug addiction in some ways reflected a changing situation in Hollywood. One of the ways of countering the threat of television was through dealing with controversial areas that the newer medium as yet was not liberated enough to treat. Another way was through the exploitation of wide-screen. Unfortunately, neither of these seemed to have helped *A Hatful of Rain* very much.

The drugs theme had been anticipated by Otto Preminger's successful film, *The Man with the Golden Arm* (1955), with its intriguing casting of Frank Sinatra as the addict and its jazzy, highly influential Elmer Bernstein score. Zinnemann's film had a more modest cast, and a bleakly economical score by Bernard Herrmann which, although contributing intelligently to the wintry atmosphere of the film, clearly did not have the commercial drive of Bernstein's music. (Herrmann had a reputation for being an abrasive and difficult man to deal with, but he and Zinnemann had needed only one perfectly amicable meeting to discuss the score, and they were mutually satisfied with the result.) When *A Hatful of Rain*, came out, its subject seemed much less explosive. It arrived amidst a crop of films such as Andre de Toth's *Monkey on My Back*

(1957) and, slightly later, Don Siegel's *The Line-Up* (1958) which had the drugs racket as its central theme. In *A Hatful of Rain* the theme of addiction seems to become less central as the film develops, but contemporary audiences, particularly because of the delayed and rather coy disclosure of what is wrong with the central character, might have had a distinct feeling of over-familiarity with such material.

The wide-screen did not seem to add much to the excitement of *A Hatful of Rain*. There is a nice moment when one of Mother's henchmen rings Johnny (Don Murray) from a bar, and the darkened phone booth at the corner of the frame is suddenly illuminated, locating very precisely the dramatic center of the scene. But, for the most part, the wide-screen tends inadvertently to emphasize the theatricality of the original. The opening-out of the film is minimal and only fitfully successful. The small scene at the typing pool, where Celia (Eva Marie Saint) seems understandably distracted, is a cumbersome inclusion that adds nothing to an understanding of her situation. On the other hand, the atmosphere of a dark, chilly New York—a correlative to the chill felt in the bones of the addict—is well conveyed. The scene where Johnny roams the streets in search of money to buy drugs is powerfully done and relevant to the theme: a flight from self that can only lead to frustration.

Like the central male characters in *Act of Violence* and *Teresa*, Johnny Pope is a person with a guilty secret. As in *Teresa*, he has been traumatized by his war experience, and the crowding in of his family—his brother, his father—is affecting his relationship with his wife. Also, as in *Teresa*, there is a kind of "mother complex." The absence of the mother in the family has led to the two brothers, Johnny and Polo (Anthony Franciosa), being brought up in an orphanage, a situation about which Polo still feels bitter. Celia is an expectant mother, and also often forced into the situation of "mothering" Polo. The sub text of the film seems to be the "search for the mother" (evocative of *The Search*) whose absence has prevented both brothers from fully growing up. This search is grotesquely perverted into Johnny's ultimate dependence on "Mother," the dope peddler, who is the only one who can provide Johnny with the peace he needs. As with the character of Philip in

Time for self-reflection: Don Murray as the war veteran who has now become a drug addict in *A Hatful of Rain*, Twentieth Century–Fox, 1957.

Teresa, Johnny's maturity comes with his rejection of 'Mother' and his renewed commitment to his wife. It is only then that his life has the possibility of moving forward.

The ending of the film is somewhat like the ending of *Teresa* in its reconciliation between husband and wife, but it is even more like the ending of *The Men*. The physical problem has not been eradicated, but husband and wife draw strength from their desire to face the future together. (In a lighter but, paradoxically, more profound vein, this is also the conclusion of *The Sundowners*.) In fact, this parallel with *The Men* is a reminder that *A Hatful of Rain* is also about post-war problems and rehabilitation. Johnny's drug addiction has been caused by his horrific experience in the Korean War. He is another of Zinnemann's victims of the legacy of war.

Less overtly, the film also offers a comment on the quality of life in post–Korean War America. At one stage, Celia and Johnny's father have an animated conversation about living in "the age of the vacuum," the father humoring and condescending to his daughter-in-law, Celia becoming quite agitated about it. The phrase is a striking one about the complacent character of Eisenhower's America. One might compare *A Hatful of Rain* with the evocation of a different class of people at the same period in Douglas Sirk's *Written on the Wind* (1956), which, in the lurid colors of melodrama rather than Zinnemann's black and white realism, paints a similar picture of a dissatisfied society drowning itself in drink and drugs. Everyone in *A Hatful of Rain* seems frustrated, getting little excitement from his or her society and trapped in the kind of confused emotional relationships where love can easily sour into hatred.

Perhaps because of these more complicated sub-themes, the center of attention shifts from Johnny's situation to the character of his brother, Polo. This shift of attention has something to do with Franciosa's extremely perceptive and sympathetic characterization (much the best performance of the film). It is also attributable to the dramatic complexity of that character's situation: a resentment against his father and yet a desire for his love; loyalty to his brother and yet envy of the devotion Johnny inspires from Celia. There is a scene in the elevator when Polo, taking Johnny to his rendezvous with the drug pushers, has almost literally to hold his brother together, a gesture that seems simultaneously an embrace and an indication of the brother as burden. The process by which Polo finally comes to recognize his own situation—that he must find his own identity and not simply be his brother's keeper—seems much more inward and interesting than the more obvious, externalized difficulties of his brother. Unfortunately, this rather dilutes the film's central situation and one's sympathy for the main character.

The resolution is rather listless. Perhaps all along it has just been too easy to elicit sympathy for a junkie when he happens to be a war hero as well. The capture of a drug pusher by the police in a children's playground makes for quite a tense scene (as elsewhere in the film and in Zinnemann's work, children are always stumbling awkwardly into a frightening adult world). But the "suspense" of Johnny's keeping his condition secret from his wife (not an easy thing to conceal, surely), and "Mother"'s change of heart at the end, are dramatic contrivances which no longer seem

Polo (Anthony Franciosa) in tense conversation with his pregnant sister-in-law (Eva Marie Saint), watched by his father (Lloyd Nolan). From *A Hatful of Rain*.

convincing. More compelling are typical tense exchanges in bare, forbidding stairwells; the ambivalent emotions that rend a typical family; the evocation of the grayness of contemporary urban life. After a "Crime Does Not Pay," it is the nearest Zinnemann came to a gangster film (and the first shot of Henry Silva, as he emerges out of the night, is memorably menacing). But it is essentially an inner drama, in which a tortured and taciturn protagonist has to find the solution to his problems not through drugs, drink, money, violence, but in himself. The Zinnemann themes are all there, but the focus seems a little blurred.

The Sundowners *(1960)*

> This is good country for sheep and not bad for men. But it's hard on us women. We never get anything out of it.

> The men come here because of the sheep and we come here because of the men. And most of us women finish up looking like the sheep. Wrinkled faces, knotty hair, not even much of a mind of our own.
> —Jon Cleary, *The Sundowners*

> Men, the men I meet here in this pub, ain't got much but what they can pick up from day to day. I believe in letting 'em have all the fun they can get while they can get it. They battle all their lives, working like slaves just to stay ahead of nature and what it can do to you, never having a holiday, keeping this part of the country alive, and when they're dead, they're forgotten.
> —Jon Cleary, *The Sundowners*

Fred Zinnemann had been asked if he were interested in making a film in and about Australia and had read and enjoyed Jon Cleary's novel, *The Sundowners*, which seemed ideal material for the screen. He agreed to make it for Warners, serving as producer-director, before spending three months on reconnaissance, seeking appropriate locations in the outback and elsewhere. When the film started shooting late in 1959, the crew encountered extreme weather conditions: rain and sleet in the Snowy River Mountains of New South Wales, boiling heat and scorching winds in the Port Augusta area of South Australia where the sheep-shearing sequences were filmed. In fact, the weather turned out to be less of a problem than the sheep. The company had acquired 5,000 of them for the droving scenes and found them more resistant to direction than the most temperamental star. Actors might be cattle, according to Alfred Hitchcock, but Zinnemann found that sheep were no actors. "In order to direct sheep," he said, "one had to learn to think like a sheep." In the end he was reduced to nominating one sheep as a sort of assistant director, who could then lead the rest. A recording of bleats and "baas," amplified in stereo, was also devised to coax the animals into camera range.

For the sheep-shearing scenes, the actors were given intensive instruction. Robert Mitchum became quite expert. On the surface, Mitchum might seem odd casting as the wanderlust Paddy Carmody, and he certainly is nothing like the physical description of Paddy in the novel. At one time Gary Cooper was being considered for the role, but illness forced him out of the running. In the event, everyone was happy with Mitchum, whose ease in his scenes with Deborah Kerr (the two had worked happily together previously on *Heaven Knows, Mr. Allison*) is so essential to conveying the warmth of the relationship between husband and wife, which is the film's main theme. Jon Cleary suggested in a letter to me that "Mitchum had the right look of larceny in his eyes for Paddy." For Zinnemann, the association was very satisfying: "He was one of the funniest men I have ever met, with the air of not caring very much, of being easily bored. He once told me that sometimes he'd like to go through a film with his eyes closed, but with the pupils painted on those heavy eyelids! But he is a first rate actor."

Having already directed her to splendid effect in *From Here to Eternity*, Zinnemann knew the dedication and talent he could rely on from Deborah Kerr in the role of the drover's wife, Ida. In some ways, the most telling example of their cooperation comes in a scene in which the actress does not say a word. Seated on the wagon, having just escaped from a forest fire, hot and covered in dust, Ida glances over to a waiting train and sees a well-groomed lady powdering her nose. The starkness of the contrast between them and their exchange of looks—disdain from the lady on the train, longing from the drover's wife—are sufficient to reduce Ida to tears. "Deborah Kerr did it beautifully," Jon Cleary told me. "That scene originally was a page of dialogue between Ida and Paddy. Fred kept working on me till finally all we had was one line: 'What's the matter, Ida?' from the puzzled Paddy. In that scene Fred taught me what the camera can do."

The gaiety of the film was undoubtedly enriched by the casting of Peter Ustinov, who gives one of his most effective screen performances as Venneker, the haughty English remittance man who becomes the Carmodys' closest friend. In the novel, Venneker is tall and bony, but the dialogue was adjusted to comment on Ustinov's physical appearance (for example, Venneker's remark to young Sean Carmody that he is growing wider while Sean is growing taller, or his later description of himself to Ida as an "elderly turtle" with a "hard shell and soft belly"). The admirable cast was completed by Glynis Johns, as the landlady of the local pub with an eye on Venneker; Michael Anderson, Jr. (son of the film director), as Sean; and a host of familiar British and Australian faces that contribute so much to reflecting the feel of the country.

Although Isobel Lennart was credited with the screenplay, she only wrote the first draft, and the major part of the writing was done by the novel's author, Jon Cleary. (The Writers Guild should have negotiated a credit on Cleary's behalf but were on strike at the time and Warners, who wanted Lennart for another commitment, never contacted him. Although disappointed, he much appreciated a gesture of Lennart's: When the script was nominated for an Oscar, she rang him up to say that she would give him credit if it won. In fact, it did not.) It is a very skillful realization of the novel in film terms, eliminating some of the novel's characterization, tightening and simplifying the final chapters, and giving firm dramatic form to moments only recorded in passing in the original (like Ida's scene at the station, or the powerful moment, very well prepared for in the film, when she strikes Paddy across the face). Cleary worked very happily with Zinnemann, appreciating the director's concern on consulting him over every change in the script, and feeling that he had perceived something essential in the material that had been missed by most critics. "The book was written partly to show a boy's crossing the frontier between childhood and adulthood," Cleary told me, (similar in theme to *The Member of the Wedding*), "but also to show the 'mateship' between a man and a woman in a marriage. The Australian tradition has been to show such mateship as existing only between men—I tried for another dimension and Fred was, I think, the first to see what I was aiming for."

Although well-received by the press, the film was not as great a success as hoped. Perhaps it was a little ahead of its time. Its unhurried evocation of an unfamiliar lifestyle was to anticipate films of the New Australian Cinema of the 1970s such as *Sunday Too Far Away* and *The Irishman*, but must have seemed rather gentle and formless for the audiences of the day. (It also anticipated Nicolas Roeg's *Walkabout*; interestingly, Roeg was a camera operator on his film.) There seems also to have been some confusion about the best way to sell it, a poster finally being produced that seemed to imply *The Sundowners* was a sex film (drawing on the tender and perfectly natural night scenes between husband and wife in the film, where there is clearly still a strong sexual attraction between them). That selling approach disappointed the sex customers, and family-minded people stayed away. In fact, *The Sundowners* is not only a family film, it is a film about family.

Although Ida and Paddy are devoted to each other, there is a conflict between them. Ida wants somewhere permanent to settle: Paddy, in the words of the novel, wants only "Ida, and the boy, and to keep moving." It is this conflict which provides the film's dramatic core, and variations on the theme are provided as the Carmodys encounter other married couples who are struggling with similar problems (the society wife of Paddy's boss who is having difficulty in settling down; the wife of one of Paddy's workmates who, although pregnant, travels a long distance to ensure she is with her husband when the child is born). Rupe Venneker (Ustinov) is an extension of Paddy, believing that most places are only good for arrivals and departures ("It could be you talking" says Ida to Paddy). Even the scene where Venneker grows violent when Carmody's dog won't let go of his leg has its point to make. Venneker, like Paddy, does not like anyone or anything tying him down or snapping at his heels.

Typically, Zinnemann is even-handed in his treatment of the two characters, making us understand the validity of both points of view and finding appropriate imagery to bring their feelings to dramatic life. Ida's hopes for the future are contained in the jam jar holding their savings which dominates one particular scene where they discuss the future of their boy. It is homely but fragile and subject to Paddy's whims, like Ida herself. Paddy is seen at his most characteristic in the outdoors when riding after a dingo to protect the sheep. Ida responds to the interiors, but the camera lights up at the landscape, and there is an intriguing tension between the feelings of domicility tenderly expressed by the most articulate and sympathetic character in the film, Ida, and yet the majesty of the outdoors to which Paddy and the audience are instinctively drawn.

Paddy is another Zinnemann outsider, wanting to resist as long as possible the ties of conventional society and the oppression of a fixed home. One could imagine him as a surrogate for the film director: moving from location to location, restless in one

The Carmody family in *The Sundowners*: Paddy (Robert Mitchum), Ida (Deborah Kerr), and their son Sean (Michael Anderson, Jr.). Whereas Ida wants to settle down, Paddy just wants "Ida, and the boy, to keep moving."

place, an adventurer challenging nature, but at the same time recognizing the strains on his family and his absolute desire to keep the family together. The film's main concerns—the security of a marriage that can hold under adversity, the belief that constancy of belonging together is more important than any amount of possessions—are handled with maturity and affection, and the imagery underlines the themes with great understanding. For example, the bush fire, which Paddy and Ida encounter early on in the film, is not simply a piece of local color. It is a metaphor for a marriage between two people who will go through fire for each other.

The emphasis on landscape and local detail, the marriage between the Irishman and the fiery red-haired heroine, the boisterous knock-about fist fights between the sheep-shearers, help to give *The Sundowners* something of the relaxed charm and flavor of John Ford's *The Quiet Man* (1952). If it retains a particular affection in one's mind, the reason is the ease and good humor with which it surveys themes and situations which the director has treated seriously elsewhere. Both Paddy and Ida are anxious to make amends to each other at the end, Paddy even offering to sell their precious horse to compensate for his squandering away the money Ida had saved for the house. "I don't want to live with a martyr," says Ida bluntly (a refreshing statement for a Zinnemann heroine!). The horse is disqualified anyway, rendering Paddy's generosity irrelevant, and this produces another of Ida's quips at the typical Zinnemann hero: "There goes both our chances to be noble!" A man offers a measly £25 for the race horse which sets off Paddy and Ida into gales of laughter, producing what the director very nicely called his "*Sierra Madre* ending"—the triumphant laughter that is a victory over life's ironies. Says Venneker severely to the man: "Twenty five pounds? Lucky for you we've got a sense of humor."

Fred Zinnemann's films have often been attacked for lacking humor. But *The Sundowners* goes some way to answering that criticism: in Ida's good-natured irony and sarcasm; in the scare over Carmody's "mad dog," counter pointed by the two old drunks musing disinterestedly over their beer, and where the crowd scatter and even the cows are seen to back away; in Venneker's linguistic pomposity; in the rhythmic slurping of soup as the drovers test Ida's suitability as cook; in the sheep-shearing contest where Carmody is beaten by a wily old weasel (Wylie Watson) who scarcely raises a sweat; even in the asides at the race track, where one compulsive gambler, on hearing that the result of the Carmody race is in doubt pending a steward's inquiry, is heard to say, "I'll bet on the protest!" Finely photographed by Jack Hildyard and invigoratingly scored by Dimitri Tiomkin, *The Sundowners* is one of Zinnemann's most deeply pleasurable films. There is a sense throughout of relaxation without slackness, affection without sentimentality. The film ends as serenely as it has opened, with Paddy and Ida on the road—the nomadic couple who own hardly anything but the clothes on their backs but whose real home is each other.

CHAPTER FIVE

State of Terror

Behold a Pale Horse *(1964)*

> And I looked, and behold a pale horse:
> And his name that sat on him was Death,
> And Hell followed with him.
> —*Book of Revelation*, Chapter 6, Verse 8

Although of different levels of achievement, three of Fred Zinnemann's later films—*Behold a Pale Horse, The Day of the Jackal* and *Julia*—have interesting similarities. All three films can be seen as the response of a civilized liberal democrat to a modern world of increasing barbarity and political totalitarianism. Ostensibly thrillers, they are chiefly films about politics and principles. Although all are set in the past, the material of each has relevance and intriguing parallels of our own times. All of them traverse backwards and forwards across different European locations, cumulatively building up a picture of the turmoil Europe has experienced in the twentieth century (Nazi tyranny in Germany, Civil War in Spain, terrorist tensions in France). The three films also have a similar structure. Each builds towards a climactic meeting or confrontation between two main characters who throughout the film have been separated by distance and by ideology (Manuel and the Police Chief in *Behold a Pale Horse*; the detective and the "Jackal" in *The Day of the Jackal* and, in a different way, Lillian and Julia in *Julia*). The three films deal with terrorism and acts against the State, actions that are seen to be either anachronistic (as in *Pale Horse*), mercenary (in *Jackal*) or courageous (in *Julia*). *Behold a Pale Horse* and *The Day of the Jackal* have identical imagery at one point: the moment when the prey is lined up in the sights of the assassin's gun, with the latter realizing that one shot will be his only chance at the long-pursued target. It is a chilling image because it brings the specter of political assassination, so much a part of the contemporary historical scene, vividly into focus.

Of the three films, *Behold a Pale Horse* is generally regarded as the least successful. Zinnemann had liked the story (it was based on a novel by Emeric Pressburger); the characterization was varied; and the themes of courage and conviction generally were of the order to stimulate his best work. He had a good technical crew and the opportunity to alternate studio work in Paris with location work in the Pyrenees and near Biarritz. The ingredients all seemed promising but mysteriously the mixture failed to rise. Why?

Zinnemann was very frank about the failure: "I made an elementary mistake. As a documentarian, I should have known that one does not have the right to expect the audience to be acquainted with the subject matter and background to the story. I assumed people would know a lot about the Spanish Civil War, and they didn't, so the characters and situation made little sense to them. I ought to have sensed this myself and insisted on adjustments in the script, but I failed to see it."

This is a forgivable failure, and Zinnemann was sometimes concerned by the lack of historical sense in modern film audiences (he told me about receiving a disturbing letter from a friend, the director Laszlo Benedek, who mentioned that he had been teaching a class on *Julia* and that a number of his students had failed to understand the scene where Vienna University is raided by the Nazis because the Swastika armbands were not visible). But the actual shooting of *Behold a Pale Horse* was for the most part not a happy experience. Although it is a well-photographed film,

Zinnemann had little patience with a cameraman who needed 45 minutes to light a close-up, while all the energy of the actors was being dissipated. He was also sensing at the time that the chemistry of the casting seemed wrong. Anthony Quinn had wanted to play the part of the Spanish guerrilla, Manuel, but the director persuaded him to play the part of the police chief, Vinolas, and he gives a modestly conceived, disciplined performance. Unfortunately, the casting of Gregory Peck as Manuel Artiguez is not quite convincing enough. The part of Manuel Artiguez requires a character performance. Although Peck is to be admired for his refusal in any way to sentimentalize the character (Zinnemann's fear that the casting of Peck might have had the effect of glamourizing terrorism at a particularly unfortunate time is, for the most part, unfounded), he brings heroic associations from previous performances which confuse the outline of the character.

Perhaps, as a subconscious reaction to the feeling that the film was not working on a human level, Zinnemann told me he felt he went overboard on the externals, and was especially self-indulgent on the Lourdes section of the film. Sometimes, as if to compensate for a feeling of uneasiness with the material (it happens also in parts of *Teresa*), his visual style becomes more highly charged, his usual self-effacing economy moving uncharacteristically towards the baroque. This has a fascination of its own, of course. Although *Behold a Pale Horse* never fully engages the imagination, it never ceases to stimulate the visual sense: in the Lourdes section, all mysterious shapes and shadows; in the boy's early journey through winding streets in his search for Artiguez; in one tremendous travelling shot towards the mountains that separate Artiguez and Vinolas, a shot that simultaneously links two disparate sequences, offers a concise indication of the distance that separates the two antagonists and thrillingly promises the confrontation to come.

Columbia Pictures must have been particularly disappointed with the film, which had restrained, respectful reviews but made no money. It had a team that brought associations with *Lawrence of Arabia* (actors Quinn and Omar Sharif; composer Maurice Jarre). Its two co-stars had recently headed the cast of one of Columbia's biggest ever successes, *The Guns of Navarone*. In fact, the advertising campaign was rather similar to *Navarone*, placing the stress on suspense and excitement and thus doubling the frustration of an audience keyed up for colorful adventure. (Because Zinnemann's films are difficult to categorize, they were difficult to advertise as well, and a number of them seemed to suffer from insensitive selling which misled audiences.) To cap everything, the film ran into trouble in Spain for its effrontery in showing a Spanish police chief as a man with a mistress and who takes bribes, and Columbia had to close its offices in Madrid.

Reflecting on the film later, Zinnemann was more philosophical and told me he was inclined to think it had been a valuable lesson: "Failure is a necessary and even a positive part of our business. It does force you to reassess and to analyze the reasons for your mistakes. Curiously, I think the failure of *Pale Horse* contributed to the success of *A Man for All Seasons*, because, when I came to that, I made absolutely certain that no one in the audience would be unclear about the background, the situation and the issues involved. I was not about to make that mistake again!"

Nevertheless, although a flawed film, it is one of some distinction. It is not so much a failed drama: rather a drama about failure. Part of its lack of commercial success could be attributed to one of its virtues, namely, the honesty with which the subject is handled and which must lead inevitably to a pessimistic outcome. The film is gradually overwhelmed by a sense of futility which would hardly endear it to popular audiences but which seems unusual and brave in the context of a Hollywood cinema generally dedicated to the pursuit of happiness.

At the time, it seemed to be regarded as a rather old-fashioned film, a '50s narrative colored by a '30s political consciousness. Seen from a more modern perspective, the film, if anything, looks ahead of its time. It anticipates films as advanced and complex as Alain Resnais' *La Guerre Est Finie* (1966) and Joseph Losey's *Roads to the South* (1979), which similarly deal with an exiled freedom fighter from the days of the Spanish Civil War who is now wavering between idealism and cynicism and is increasingly in conflict with what he sees as the simplistic revolutionary politics of the young. Part of the interest of *Behold a Pale Horse* is precisely the way it places the legacy of a 1930s political idealism in the context of an atmosphere that has something of a post–1956 fatalism and the feeling, to quote John Osborne's young man in *Look Back in Anger*, that "there are no good causes left."

The film begins with some newsreel footage of the end of the Spanish Civil War in 1939. It has the stamp of realism one recognizes from a Zinnemann film and is a reminder of the '30s documentary tradition which provided him with some of his cinematic roots. It is then somewhat surprising to see Gregory Peck as Manuel Artiguez emerging from this footage, showing obvious reluctance in surrendering his weapons and plainly resistant to the idea that the struggle is over. The imposition of Peck's star presence on this grainily authentic footage is technically skillful but ostensibly incongruous. Yet it is appropriate that Artiguez looks awkward here. Like More in *A Man for All Seasons*, he is a man out of step with history, who thus refuses to accommodate himself to historical inevitability. The refusal of Peck's star presence to integrate itself into the documentary fatalism of the vanquished fighters against Fascism sets up the atmosphere for the entire film, in which Artiguez will make a defiant anachronistic star gesture in an endeavor to reaffirm his legendary valor. Artiguez's slow recovery of self-respect comes through a chain of events unleashed by a boy Paco (Marietto Angeletti), who has heard of Artiguez's exploits during the Civil War and wants him to avenge his father's death by killing Artiguez's old adversary, Captain Vinolas.

As Paco is preparing to cross the border on his mission to Artiguez, he spots a bull in a field and, almost instinctively, calls "Toro!" in a gesture of challenge. The metaphor of the bullfight is to inform the structure of the whole film. Captain Vinolas will play matador to Artiguez's aging bull. He will taunt and provoke him, baiting a trap into which Artiguez will eventually charge, but he will let others, like picadors, finish the job. Vinolas is not so complex a character as Artiguez but he is seen in rather similar ways, which emphasizes a mysterious bond between them (even if, structurally speaking, it is a mistake to keep them apart for so long: we have to take their mutual enmity very much on trust). Like Artiguez, Vinolas is insecure and particularly mistrustful of the young who seem not to give him the respect he deserves and seem also to be preying on his position. Just as Artiguez uses violence to get what he wants, so Vinolas exploits the opportunities of his position for corruption and intimidation, first being seen on a pale horse which he will covertly claim as a bribe. Like Artiguez, he is a man who seems to need sexual reassurance to guard against the onset of age. They are both old men living on their memories, notably their hatred for each other, which seems the main thing keeping them alive. The similarity between them strengthens the structure and gives a certain irony to their conflict.

Drawn into this private feud are the boy Paco and Father Francisco (Omar Sharif). Artiguez and his friends hate the Church, a legacy of the Civil War. To the police the Father seems little more than a tangential irritant. When the news of the death of Artiguez's mother is revealed to Vinolas and the traitor Carlos (a very fine cameo from Raymond Pellegrin), the two men quite forget that Father Francisco is present and might feel some moral obligation to reveal their murderous plan to Artiguez. It is a foretaste of the futility of Father Francisco's actions in the film and indeed of the ending, where he is an observer through a barred window, stranded and forgotten. Captain Vinolas visits the church at one stage, but his prayers have nothing to do with religion and a lot to do with superstition and fear.

Father Francisco is initially hesitant about warning Artiguez of the trap: He has been preparing for his pilgrimage to Lourdes. "I know it's a sacred duty," he says when he learns that Artiguez's dying mother wishes to see him, "but surely if you can explain to her...." A recurrent motif of the whole film is one of frustrated or frustrating journeys. Father Francisco really wants to go to Lourdes but, at the crucial moment, fate inserts a cruel wedge between desire and duty: However reluctantly, the priest knows that there is only one path he can follow. This will apply equally to Artiguez: He will meander and equivocate, but he knows ultimately that there is only one road he can take. It is in this context of broken journeys, wanderings and metaphysical search that the scene at Lourdes, where Artiguez and the boy search for the priest to confirm the boy's story that Carlos is the traitor, takes on an additional dimension. It fits quite appropriately into a film whose digressive patterns and unexpected diversions parallel the confused purposes of the characters whose lives are being tossed in unpredictable directions.

The child, the traitor, the friend and the priest all, at different stages, come into Artiguez's small, dark room and whisper different, contradictory messages to him, reassessing and reactivating his past. It is as if the room were his head, his conscience, for which each visitor has a message. The traitor, now unmasked but having escaped, offers the temptation of action: Should Artiguez go back and face certain death? The priest brings a stirring perhaps of Artiguez's former idealism that has been eroded by age. Paco brings back to his consciousness the spirit of his youth and a revival of tender feeling. His friend Pedro (Paolo Stoppa) is a witness and a reminder of the man Artiguez was. There is an unemphatic moment when the friend enters the room and Artiguez questioningly pats Pedro's pot-belly. Pedro just shrugs, in a gesture that clearly means, "It's age, it catches up with all of us...," a gesture, moreover, that is thematically crucial.

Artiguez journeys alone on a bus to meet Pedro, joining him on a remote hill outside a secluded café. Artiguez knows that his mother is dead, that Carlos is a traitor, that a trap has been laid—and that he must return. "What else can I do?" he says, before adding slyly, "besides, they don't think that I can." This feeling of defiant bravado carries on briefly into the following scene, when Artiguez goes into the cafe to pay the young waitress and there is momentarily a spark of sexual attraction between them. But desire gives way to relief when the moment passes. It is a poignant farewell to youth and a recognition on Artiguez's part that he should not mistake the will for the deed. In a way the moment anticipates the whole of the finale, in which Manuel's action is a symbolic and personal gesture of farewell rather than any meaningful act of political terrorism. This small scene with the waitress is perhaps the strongest, the most moving in the film, changing from a scene charged with sexual expectation to one saturated with an atmosphere of death.

From this point the narrative increases in tension, accentuated by Maurice Jarre's score which has been uncommonly alert to the subtle gradations of tempo and tension. A slow farewell to the mountains, stunningly photographed by Jean Badal, leads to an encounter on the road between Manuel and a driver who is to betray him to the police. To this character and to most others in the film, Artiguez is an anachronism not a legend, a reward not a cause. Artiguez has to put on spectacles to break open a lock and enter a building and he looks round furtively, as if he is more afraid of being seen wearing glasses—an indelible sign of age—than of actually being apprehended. His overpowering of the guard is a noisy affair, for Artiguez is now clumsy and tired, and the shoot-out, like that of *High Noon*, is realistically, convincingly messy. He nevertheless has time for one last affirmative act of protest against the police state. When unexpectedly faced with the choice of shooting adversary or informer—for a Zinnemann character a typical anguished choice of infinite complexity, involving an assessment of what one wants to do against what one *must* do—Artiguez makes an instinctively moral decision. He shoots the informer.

The finale is nicely detailed. A foreign reporter angers Vinolas by referring to Artiguez as a "bandit" and not as a "political enemy," and seeming therefore to undervalue the Captain's achievement. (The reporter is played by Michel Lonsdale, one of a number of performers in Zinnemann films—Rod Steiger, Vanessa Redgrave, Lambert Wilson—who graduated from small roles to much more important parts in later films.) Otherwise the police seem to have the press and the people completely under control. Artiguez's gesture has certainly not reactivated any of the emotions or the causes for which he fought. The people filing past his body seem passive and the police car drives contemptuously through the crowd, the power of the State pushing to one side the cowed population it controls. Yet there is an element of doubt amid the police celebrations, and the ending is another Fred Zinnemann question mark. "Why did he come back?" asks Vinolas and the question echoes ironically, giving a hollow ring to the Captain's victory.

Maybe Artiguez's gesture has been politically futile, but not personally so. There is a revealing moment when Father Francisco has written an important note to Artiguez but, in Artiguez's absence, has left it with Paco. Instinctively mistrustful of the priest, Paco tears up the note and tries to flush it down the toilet. It resurfaces—as inconvenient truths have a habit of doing. Artiguez would like to wash away his past ("What is it they want?" he asks early on, "I've done enough"). But sooner or later, self-respect, conscience and responsibility must resurface, however hard he tries to

Manuel Artiquez (Gregory Peck) lines up the informer in his sights in *Behold a Pale Horse*, Columbia Pictures, 1964.

push them down. He cannot deny them without also denying who he is, what he has been. Once he has recognized and accepted that, his fate is sealed, but his character redeemed.

The Day of the Jackal *(1973)*

> "If the Jackal wasn't Calthrop," said Thomas after Calthrop had finally walked out of the door a free man, "then who the hell was he?"
> —Frederick Forsyth, *The Day of the Jackal*

"There's nothing as timid as a million dollars." This is a maxim about the film industry which applies to those financiers who are prepared to invest money in a film but only with a form of insurance, preferably a star name. But some films not only do not need stars, but would actually suffer from their inclusion. As Zinnemann said mischievously on one occasion, "I'm sure if the financiers had had their way, they would have cast Frank Sinatra as Gandhi."

With *The Day of the Jackal*, Zinnemann encountered considerable resistance to his proposal of Edward Fox in the leading role, even though a certain box office appeal was already apparent from the runaway success of the novel (a factor which certainly influenced the selling of the film). But could a big-budget film like this succeed without stars? Zinnemann's argument about this was that the Jackal *had* to be a person whose face was not instantly recognizable and who could melt convincingly into a crowd. Put a star in that role and this chameleon-like capacity would no longer be convincing and an audience would not believe it. Fox was an ideal choice in other ways. It was an example of the kind of casting against type that Zinnemann particularly liked, Fox at that time being principally known to cinema audiences for his impeccably aristocratic performance in *The Go-Between* (1971). Fox had addition qualities which fitted perfectly Zinnemann's concept of the Jackal: "My idea of the Jackal was that he was a privileged Englishman gone wrong, and I wanted someone who could convey breeding, ruthless coldness, also an intelligence, an enormous sharpness of mind."

Zinnemann had stumbled across the project almost by accident. He was in the office of producer John Woolf one day, discussing a film of *Abelard and Heloise*, for which they were having difficulty in finding the right script and cast. There was a parcel on Woolf's desk and Fred asked him what it was. "The galleys of a new novel, *The Day of the Jackal*," Woolf replied. "The publishers think it's going to be very big and I've an option on the film rights." Zinnemann asked him if he could read it and, having done so, asked if he could film it.

The attraction of the material for Zinnemann stemmed basically from a fascination with it as a technical challenge. The material was essentially visual rather than verbal, which would certainly be a change from his previous completed film, *A Man for All Seasons*. It was a large-scale work giving the opportunity for spectacular set-pieces (notably the attempt on de Gaulle's life on Liberation Day) of a kind that Zinnemann had not attempted for a long time. The film's first assistant director, Alain Bonnot, commented most interestingly to me on the mechanics of putting a scene like this together. "If I have a crowd scene of a hundred people," he said, "I don't split it into 50 men and 50 women: I divide the number into three schoolteachers, two bank clerks, a soldier, and so forth. It's not only a guide to the wardrobe department, it helps the extras themselves to contribute a characterization." Bonnot told me that Zinnemann, who had chosen to shoot this scene on the busiest National Holiday—the 14th of July—because of the grandiose military parade, seemed to revel in the organizational complexity. One thing that helped was having the full cooperation of the French police, granted because, according to the director: "They were under the impression that the film showed them in a good light: They got their man!"

The main challenge was to involve an audience in a story of which they already knew the outcome. Everyone knows that de Gaulle was not assassinated; could an effective suspense film be made from the assassination attempt, given the further difficulty that the central character is not one with whom an audience could identify? *The Day of the Jackal* was, then, a technical exercise in a very specific sense: Its success would be dependent essentially on its *technique*. The weight of interest could not be on narrative

The English tourist on a deadly mission: Edward Fox as the assassin in *The Day of the Jackal*, Universal 1973.

uncertainty nor on characterization. Everything would depend on *how* the story is told.

To maintain interest, the film first adopts an entertaining variety of tone, tempo and technique. It sweeps through a series of locations—Paris, London, Vienna, Genoa—as it follows the arc of the narrative and attempts to involve an audience in the thrill of the chase. The violence is sometimes explicit in the modern manner (the torture of Welensky) or inexplicit in the classical manner (the murder of Colette is conveyed simply through her hand going limp, rather like the famous ending of *All Quiet on the Western Front*, the film that gave Zinnemann his first job in Hollywood).

In addition to violence, there is also humor, but that too is varied and sometimes lethal, as in the moment when the Jackal shares a joke with the Italian forger before felling him with a deadly karate blow. At other stages, the humor is more ironical, as in the moment when the pompous British police official (Donald Sinden) suddenly realizes that he is speaking to the Prime Minister on the phone, or the scene when the French Government minister airily dismisses the detective as being no longer required, only to have to recall him later and sheepishly admit that the Jackal has slipped through their fingers. The latter joke is continued by removing the Jackal from the film for fully seven minutes at a time when an audience is most curious to know where he is, namely in the build-up to de Gaulle's arrival for the presentation of medals on Liberation Day. Yet, for all the ironical humor here, this final set-piece is also a tour-de-force of suspense, cross-cutting between the police, the assassin and the prey with such skill that an audience is prevented from leaping ahead to the foregone conclusion but becomes caught up excitedly in the film's sense of present time.

There is an element of play also about the film's obsessive close-ups of clocks, which seem designed to outnumber those of *High Noon*. Both *High Noon* and *The Day of the Jackal* are about races against time. But whereas the close-ups of the clock in *High Noon* emphasize the urgency of the Marshal's situation, in *The Day of the Jackal* such shots seem cerebral and often funny. The clocks are different from each other, wittily suggesting through their sometimes plain, sometimes ornate design the owner and the location to which they belong. Such close-ups certainly wind up the action of the film and allude to the precision of the Jackal's plan (he always seems to catch trains just as they are about to depart, as if everything has been calculated to the minute). But their main function is to emphasize the film itself as a skilful mechanism.

The audience is deliberately detached from any close identification with any of the characters. It is a thriller, shot in the style of a newsreel, with people seeming little more than pieces in an elaborate game of chess, a feeling enhanced by the absence of star names (an absence which Zinnemann felt would add to the realism). The film's considerable technical virtuosity is all devoted to an overall atmosphere of dark abstraction. Ralph Kemplen's dazzling editing fragments the action in a way that seems to emphasize objects more than events and people. Jean Tournier's photography is so coldly lucid that it seems to chill the action. The usually melodic Georges Delerue contributes a score in which portentous rhythm is given precedence over theme. There is a correlation between the film's clockwork precision and that of the Jackal. If the film emphasizes method over motive, technique over content, means over ends, so does the Jackal, whose only concern is with the successful accomplishment of a professional job. The style *is* the character, which is precisely the reason that it has the capacity to disturb.

The Day of the Jackal occupied a very interesting place in the cinema of the 1970s. It is, with *Five Days One Summer*, perhaps the most original and unusual film in Zinnemann's career. It could be grouped with other distinguished films of the time, such as Gillo Pontecorvo's *The Battle of Algiers* (1966), Costa-Gavras's *Z* (1968), Claude Chabrol's *Nada* (1972) and Richard Lester's *Juggernaut* (1974). These were all mainstream films which highlighted in a questioning and dynamic way the implications and atmosphere of terrorism, assassination and political extremism in contemporary society. However, unlike these films, whose specific perceptions were informed by overtly radical sympathies, *The Day of the Jackal* observes this world of political conspiracy with a withering objectivity.

The other contemporary film tradition on which *Jackal* drew is the world of John Le Carré, as represented at that time in films such as *The Spy Who Came in from the Cold* (1965), *The Deadly Affair* (1966) and *The Looking Glass War* (1969). Part of the interest of Le Carré's work is his relation of this world of political blackmail and betrayal to the world of privilege and the Establishment. Part of the black humor of *The Day of the Jackal* derives from the *Englishness* of the Jackal's enterprise: doing all his research in the British Museum; selecting his alternative identity of Paul Oliver Duggan from the headstone of a grave in the most English of country churchyards; perfecting the forgery of his papers on a John Bull printing set. He is Raffles with a telescopic lens, combining the murderousness of the terrorist with the manners of the gentleman-tourist. One of the neatest scenes of the film is a brief one in Notre Dame Cathedral when he assesses the awesome architecture not as an aesthete but as an assassin scouting locations. Outwardly the Jackal has all the appearance of the "tourist," which is how he describes himself, but this is "tourism" put to a deadly professional purpose. Given this English connection, it is perhaps appropriate that the police are given their first lead by a

Foreign Office official whose ingenuity in spotting the connection between the name "Calthrop" and the French word for "jackal" specifically derives from that most English of talents—the ability to solve *the Times* crossword. The film's main source of humor throughout is British *hauteur* (from Whitehall bluster to Scotland Yard bureaucracy) which comes from a class arrogance that can scarcely countenance the idea of an Englishman as an enemy of the State.

If the Jackal is the negation of the blond public school hero, he is also the negation of a Fred Zinnemann hero. He is not entirely atypical. Like most of Zinnemann's leading characters, he is a loner. Also, there is a point in the film where he is faced with an urgent personal choice. When he is informed that the authorities know of the existence of the Jackal, he drives quickly away from the immediate danger and pauses briefly at a crossroad between Paris and Rome. Should he go through with the plan or cross the border into safety? Instinctively, like the Marshal in *High Noon*, like the guerrilla in *Behold a Pale Horse*, he turns back for a rendezvous with his destiny.

In every other way, the Jackal is the complete antithesis of the Zinnemann hero. If Zinnemann's most famous and characteristic films are about identity and conscience, *The Day of the Jackal* is fascinating because it is the one film with a central character who has neither. The nebulousness of the Jackal's personality is suggested through his bewildering variety of disguises, his nonchalant exchange of sexual roles, his capacity for mental and physical withdrawal and, ultimately, his epitaph, which is the film's last line: "Who the hell was he?" Also he has the perfect profession for a man without a conscience—that of a hired killer. The camera invariably stands at some distance from his killings, as if retreating from such cold-blooded inhumanity, and murder is suggested indirectly more than depicted graphically (a crash as someone falls; a cat arching its back as the Jackal prowls past after the murder of the forger; or the bizarre clatter of a lobster on the kitchen floor as the Jackal closes in on his homosexual pick-up).

For suggestive horror, the film's most extraordinary and famous scene takes place in an isolated wood where the Jackal tests the effectiveness of his rifle, using a watermelon to simulate his prospective victim's head. The sequence builds quietly and steadily through his preparations to the moment of the final shot when the bullet hits its target and the watermelon explodes. The scene gains enormous force from its contrast between pastoral peacefulness and intimations of violence; between the clinical cleanliness of the Jackal's experiment and the mess which results from its success; and particularly from the unpleasant metaphorical suggestiveness of the watermelon itself. This is what a bullet does to the human brain, that last image tells us—it turns it to red mush.

If this scene is the most memorable demonstration of indifference to life in the film, it is not an isolated example and nor are all the examples confined to the activities of the Jackal. The tone is set early on by the execution of the OAS General (Jean Sorel). "No French soldier is going to raise his rifle against me," he has declared in prison, a declaration swiftly followed by his being blindfolded, put against a tree and shot. A grim joke at his misplaced confidence perhaps, but also a bleak introduction to a world where violent betrayal becomes the norm. An OAS girl, who is being used to seduce and gain information from a French politician, is ordered to burn incriminating pictures of her fiancé: the small bonfire in the grate stands as a symbol for the cauterization of feeling necessary in this kind of work. Olga Georges-Picquot's delicate cameo brings a troubled tenderness to the scene, but the one which follows, between the Jackal and the gunsmith (Cyril Cusack), is the one which takes inhuman indifference to its most extreme point. Murder most foul is discussed with a polite, civilized formality. "Will it be a head shot or a chest shot ... and will the gentleman be moving?" Their only concern is with the technical perfection of the weapon and the victim has no more identity to them than ... a watermelon.

In the midst of such uncomfortably detached exchanges, the film inserts Zinnemann's most horrifying torture scene: the brutal interrogation of the OAS agent, Welensky. As shocking as the torture itself is the callous reaction of the police. "What did they do to the bastard?" cries the policeman as he listens to the recording of Welensky's screams, adding, "I can't understand a word!" It is not the brutality of their methods that has occasioned his outburst: It is exasperation at their inefficiency in extracting information, which makes his job more difficult. In human terms, his attitude is scarcely different from the gunsmith's. Even the most likable character in the film, the detective Lebel (Michel Lonsdale) seems to become tainted by the atmosphere of suave cynicism. Introduced first of all tending his pigeons, seeming another Maigret with a slavishly devoted wife, he gradually becomes caught up in the suspect methods of his superiors, in which results are all that matter. He authorizes secret phone tapping and pressurizes witnesses. It seems logical, then, that this initially peaceable man should dirty his own hands and be the one who finally has to blast the Jackal to pieces. The implication seems to be that terrorism can only be combated by terrorist methods from the State, which necessitates an indifference to the relation between means and ends. It is a depressing thought, for the danger is that it might ultimately blur the distinction between the two.

Accidentally perhaps, the disquieting similarity between the methods of the OAS and the forces which oppose them tends to be reinforced by the casting and by the performances. British actors are cast either as members of the British Establishment, or as French politicians, policemen or even as members of the OAS. Zinnemann told me that, on reflection, he was unhappy with this particular aspect of the film: he felt the French characters, even though played by English actors, should have been given French accents. ("John Woolf wanted this and I didn't, because I always think it sounds phony; but I think now that John was right.") Some actors make a vague shot at a French accent, others do not, and a certain confusion about whose side a person is on could well result, as Zinnemann feared. The confusion is nevertheless curiously apt. In a world of confusing appearance where State, subversive, mercenary and minister are practically indistinguishable in method, it makes sense that they are well nigh indistinguishable in manner and appearance as well.

Perhaps the scene which conveys this best is the early one between the Jackal and the OAS. It is a superbly executed scene, with some testy discussion about OAS informers and in which the most important person in the scene is the one standing outside the door, Welensky. He is there when the Englishman reveals his code name "Jackal" and that moment, unseen by any of them, is the point at which their plot is to go wrong and to result many months later in their scheme disappearing in a cloud of dust. But the striking

With the gunsmith (Cyril Cusack) in attendance, the Jackal (Edward Fox) tests his weapon. From *The Day of the Jackal*, 1973.

thing about the scene is its atmosphere. The subject under discussion is the assassination of a major world statesman, yet the topic is debated by men in smart suits behind a desk. It looks, for all the world, like businessmen conducting a job interview. It is the scene's matter-of-factness which is the truly shocking thing about it. "You simply can't afford to be emotional," says the Jackal. It is his personal credo, and ultimately everyone else's as well. Beneath the technique and the thrills of *The Day of the Jackal* lurks a disquieting fable in which torture, treachery and terrorism become the accepted currency of modern politics.

Julia *(1977)*

> Old paint on canvas, as it ages, sometimes becomes transparent. When that happens it is possible in some pictures to see the original lines: a tree will show through

> a woman's dress, a child makes way for a dog, a boat is no longer on an open sea. That is called "pentimento" because the painter "repented," changed his mind....
>   The paint has aged now and I wanted to see what was there for me once, what is there for me now.
> —Lillian Hellman, *Pentimento*

Julia is a remembrance of things past. Yet it seems a very modern film in the way in which it is constructed. Its use of narration is extremely sophisticated in its awareness of the partiality and selectiveness of point of view: It tells us as much about the narrator as about the events. Walter Murch's remarkable editing organizes the action and the leaps in time in a challengingly complex way. (Zinnemann had chosen Murch for the job because he had been enormously impressed by his work on Coppola's *The Conversation*, and discovered, quite by chance, that Murch was equally eager to work with him.) Also the central relationship between Lillian (Jane Fonda) and Julia (Vanessa Redgrave) offers an original feminine variation on the "buddy movie" formula which was one of the principal features of Hollywood filmmaking in the '70s.

Although Sidney Pollack had originally been scheduled for the film, Zinnemann seems ideal casting. For one thing, his sensibilities have a certain kinship with those of the work's author, Lillian Hellman. Ms. Hellman was defying HUAC in 1952 at the time when Zinnemann was making *High Noon*; both could be described as liberal democrats whose work reflects the precariousness of humanist values in the face of a searching political wind. For another thing, Zinnemann's European background brought an authority and authenticity of feeling to the film's pre-war atmosphere (the tense train journey between borders, people huddling in rooms for fear of the news and the noise outside). Like *The Search*, *Julia* shows well-meaning, unsophisticated America of the '30s having to learn the fearful language of Nazi Europe.

Julia is not a realistic reconstruction of an incident in Lillian's past but an imaginative memory of it. Further, it is a memory that is informed with the hindsight of a personal feeling of failure. The film's overall tone is crucially influenced by its conclusion, which is concerned not simply with Lillian's relief in accomplishing her mission but also her failure to trace Julia's child. (The film recalls

The Search again, in its vision of the plight of children in a cruel adult world, reflected not only in the fate of Julia's child but also in Julia's estrangement from her grandparents.)

The stress on reverie and memory takes the film close to the realms of dream and the supernatural. Lillian's sensitivity to Julia's imminent danger on two occasions borders on second sight. The incident when the Nazi students run riot in Vienna University and Julia is seriously injured is prefaced by a shot of Lillian as she suddenly sits bolt upright and says her friend's name as if hit by a wave of uncanny apprehension. The murder of Julia is foreshadowed by a shot of Yorick's skull in a Moscow production of *Hamlet* which Lillian is attending, and by Hamlet's reverie for his dead friend which seems inexplicably to activate in Lillian's mind a premonition of her friend's fate. It is as if Julia is part of her subconscious. The film very cleverly conveys the sense of Julia as both solid yet spectral. Julia is talked about more than seen, and the film seems as much about Julia as an idea (or ideal) as Julia as a person.

The film's structure is associative and subjective rather than linear and chronological. This is established immediately in the film's mysterious, mesmerizing opening. For example, the third shot is of the screeching train that is to carry Lillian on her traumatic journey: Chronologically it only occurs halfway through the story; subjectively it dominates it. Douglas Slocombe's photography coats the film, pentimento-like, with a nostalgic glow over the harsh reality, as if to indicate that these are events remembered rather than recreated. (Zinnemann hired Slocombe because he needed someone who could photograph mature women and make them, when required, look like young girls, and he had been stunned by what Slocombe had achieved along these lines with Katharine Hepburn in *Love Among the Ruins*.) When Lillian is waiting tensely for news of Julia in the Vienna hospital, she remembers the two of them together in a boat and the weather is dark and overcast. When she is being rowed by Dashiell Hammett after the success of her play, the sky is clear and blue. Lillian seems instinctively to project her mood across her memory, so that the whole film is colored by it, pulling the tone between triumphant self-confidence and anxious self-recrimination.

Within this structure, then, one is never quite sure whether

Julia is fact or fantasy, a real person or a dream image with the courage and convictions which Lillian aspires to but falls short of achieving. The two are educated to a similar high level, and have a similar outlook on the world. But Julia channels her energies and intellect into the social commitment of an activist. Lillian channels hers into the self-absorption of the artist, in a way transmitting her relationship with Julia into the close female friendship of the characters in her play, *The Children's Hour*, and again, with second sight, seeming to foresee the tragic end of one of them (the play too ends in premature death, as does this story). Julia drops out of society for her beliefs. Lillian is seduced by society (she likes fame and sable coats) and has begun to dilute her beliefs as a consequence. One could see Julia, then, as Lillian's social conscience and as a projection of Lillian's sense of guilt and inadequacy, both intellectually and politically. No wonder that the dream is constantly hovering on the brink of nightmare.

The earlier childhood scenes provide something of the context of this relationship. Lillian is student to Julia's teacher in that initiation dinner on New Year's Eve with Julia's grandparents, the scene having an amusing sense of contained formality. (By the end of the film, this stiffness of the elders has hardened into something more sinister when Lillian revisits that house with the news of Julia's death.) They play word games which invariably end in defeat for Lily when Julia exploits her superiority at languages. This again anticipates Lillian's future problems as an American in Europe, having difficulty in making herself understood on the phone and being drawn into a situation where she is made to feel, physically and psychologically, a stranger in a foreign land. The two separate but keep precariously in touch by letter and phone, with always a sense that the distance between them might be growing into an ideological and not simply physical one. Julia is risking her life for the anti–Nazi cause. Lillian at this stage can only watch (observing the social unrest from her hotel) and visit (waiting to see Julia in hospital, a shot that is unmistakable Fred Zinnemann, an isolated individual in a lonely bare room that is dimly lit by a solitary light). When Julia tries to speak in hospital, Lillian cannot understand her. Everything is building to the crucial moment of the film when a stranger, Johann (Maximilian Schell), is to

A flashback scene from *Julia*, with Jane Fonda (left) as Lillian Hellman and Vanessa Redgrave as Julia.

approach her on behalf of Julia and ask her to smuggle some money into Berlin en route from Paris to Moscow.

It is a key section of the film—"where the story really begins," Zinnemann said. Johann approaches her when she is returning from an expensive dinner and night out with her friends, Alan Campbell (Hal Holbrook) and Dorothy Parker (Rosemary Murphy).

His request for food is a pointed contrast to Lillian's lifestyle, the style she might be risking if she accepts the assignment, and is also an echo perhaps of the similar deprivations of Julia herself. In the scene over breakfast, Lillian betrays her nervousness, as she does several times in the film, through a certain repetition and self-consciousness of language. (Alvin Sargent's screenplay is marvelous on details like this.) When they go outside and talk, Johann's innate gallantry, belied by his shabby appearance, is conveyed in a single gesture: Placing a napkin on the park bench so that Lillian can sit down. A gesture like that speaks volumes about the Old World courtesies that Fascism has crushed. When Johann says, "Will you help us?," he has put Lillian into a position where she must declare herself, for or against. No compromise is possible. He outlines the plan and also Julia's perception of Lillian's character which might jeopardize it. "You are afraid of being afraid, and so will do what sometimes you cannot do..." he says, "try not to be heroic." "I assure you," replies Lillian, "I would never try to be heroic."

It is the quintessential Zinnemann dilemma, the bravery of people to whom physical courage does not come easily but who recognize that to act otherwise would be to undermine the values by which they have lived. It is a severe test, for such people have a lot to lose and they could always find reasons for not doing what they instinctively know they must. Lillian is risking imprisonment and her career if she becomes involved in this: She might even be sacrificing her life. She has to think it through and it precipitates another childhood recollection of herself and Julia, that has clear connections with the present: that moment when she stumbles on the treacherous tree-path in her insistence on following Julia rather than taking the easier route. The parallel between this childhood venture and the risky enterprise she must now consider is cleverly handled. The red jumper of Lillian as a child links with her red dress as an adult, to suggest a continuity in her personality; in both situations her desire to live up to what she feels is Julia's image of her vies with her fear of being swept away. In both cases, Julia's insistence that Lillian should not do it if she does not feel she is able makes Lillian perversely more determined to go ahead. There really is no choice at all. In order to vindicate Julia's faith in her and be true to the Julia in herself, she can only act in one way.

Some additional instances of attention to detail make this point in the film even more compelling. The match which blows out during Lillian's tense conversation with Johann links with a similar motif when Lillian has been waiting anxiously for Hammett's verdict on her play. The simple word "Hello," in the moment Johann utters it here, becomes charged with foreboding. It is the codeword which indicates her acceptance of the plan when she encounters Johann at the station. Her uttering of the word is the moment the nightmare begins. Her repeating the word in her dream near the end of the film, when she screams "Hello" to Johann in the dark Berlin station, is the moment the nightmare ends. It is also the word she screams into the hollow silence of the home of Julia's grandparents when she is searching for the child. The innocent word is ominous because it means exactly the reverse of what it says. When she says it to Johann, it is actually her farewell to him, the last time she is to see him, one of the numerous farewell scenes of the film. (The whole film might be seen as an extended farewell to a particular culture and to a Europe before a holocaust from which, psychologically, it has never recovered.) It is also Lillian's temporary farewell to her comfortable bourgeois life. She crosses the border from cloistered artistic utterance to decisive political action.

The train journey is full of suspense. A train passes and Lillian is startled, the parade of flashing lights a visual metaphor for her shrill nervous fears. Throughout the film she has been startled by sharp sounds. (Assistant director Alain Bonnot caught Jane Fonda by surprise on one occasion in the scene when Lillian has left Johann in the gardens. There are some children playing and, on Bonnot's signal, they suddenly came shrieking towards Fonda, taking her by surprise, producing exactly the reaction of nervous shock that was needed for that character.) This constant state of tension builds to the terrifying point where she herself becomes a single nightmarish shriek that wakes her from her sleep—"inhabited by a cry" in Sylvia Plath's phrase. Her every movement on the train is cramped and self-conscious, a reminder that being on the train at all could jeopardize her freedom. She feels helpless, stranded and alone and this sense of isolation never leaves her on her journey. In her anxiety, she does not recognize the efforts of the two women opposite who are willing her to succeed but of whom she feels a little afraid and awed (perhaps even here, a ghostly evocation of the role of Hammett and Julia in Lillian's life). The sense of being completely alone is the image with which the film has begun and the one with which it will end, like the endings of so many of Zinnemann's films: *The Seventh Cross, The Member of the Wedding, The Nun's Story, Behold a Pale Horse, Five Days One Summer.*

The meeting with Julia is the emotional heart of the film and one of the most beautiful scenes Zinnemann ever directed. It would be difficult to overpraise the performances of Jane Fonda and Vanessa Redgrave ("direction is easy when you are working with people of such quality"). The scene economically shows the change of the characters' social and political situation: Lillian elegant, Julia casual; Lillian tremulously prosperous, Julia cheerfully crippled. It is a scene that is hushed, cramped and urgent as distinct from their other scenes together, which have been leisurely, luxurious or outdoors. Yet the friendship of a lifetime is evoked in those few highly charged minutes, partly from their slipping into a pattern of behavior and language that one recognizes from their childhood. "Listen to me. You're not listening," says Julia, to which Lillian replies, "I am listening, I am," an exchange which is a direct echo of the childhood scene between the two when Julia's social concern has first become explicit. Julia is the realist, Lillian is still the dreamer. "Put your hat on. Put your hat *on*," instructs Julia, another remembrance of Lillian's confusion on the train when she has taken out the hat (in which the money is being smuggled) and the lady opposite has said: "You would put on? You would put *on*." There is a wonderful naturalness, warmth and poignancy about the scene, Lillian apologizing for her tears and anger, Julia munching caviar as she tells Lily of her daughter (Zinnemann told me he loved Vanessa Redgrave's reading of that line, the way the naturalness of the gesture plays against the potential sentimentality of the moment).

Zinnemann's films have always been sensitive in their treatment of women, who invariably emerge not simply as romantic objects but as vibrant and intelligent human beings in their own right. They sometimes supply a strength which the man lacks, as in *Teresa* and *A Hatful of Rain*. The only person who helps the Marshal in *High*

Jason Robards as Dashiell Hammett and Jane Fonda as Lillian Hellman in *Julia*, Twentieth Century–Fox, 1977.

Noon is his wife. *From Here to Eternity, The Sundowners, Oklahoma!* and *A Man for All Seasons* have interesting things to say about the role of women in male oriented societies, and the woman's point of view is fundamental in *Five Days One Summer*. Indeed, if one thinks of *Teresa, The Member of the Wedding, The Nun's Story,*

Julia and *Five Days One Summer*, one could argue that some of Zinnemann's best films are centrally about women. This might well be a logical consequence of his scepticism about the macho American hero, but it would explain why *Julia* succeeded so well as an alternative to the Hollywood "buddy movie" genre, and why it should have been appreciated, albeit with reservations, by the feminist movement.

Some have felt that the building up of Dash Hemmett (the splendid Jason Robards) in the narrative undermines the stature of the heroine. But Hammett, like Julia, is another dimension of Lillian's conscience, another important voice in her head as she wavers in her conviction about her political beliefs on the one side, and her artistic potential on the other. Such a serious study of character and principle must have looked strange in a Hollywood at that time thrashing about with the masculine super-heroics of *Jaws* and the like. But Zinnemann was always more interested in ordinary people who know fear but have the *Zivilcourage* to overcome it. *Julia* is a supreme summation of his major themes.

CHAPTER SIX

Maidens and Mountains

Five Days One Summer *(1982)*

> I shall be telling this with a sigh
> Somewhere ages and ages hence:
> Two roads diverged in a wood, and I—
> I took the one less travelled by,
> And that has made all the difference.
> —From "The Road Not Taken," in
> Robert Frost's collection *Mountain Interval*

Two of Fred Zinnemann's passions throughout his life were movies and mountains, so it was inevitable that sooner or later they should come together. The inspiration came on a holiday in Switzerland in 1979, and particularly from his stay at the little village of Pontresina near St. Moritz which provided spectacular views of the Swiss Alps. His mind drifted back to a Kay Boyle short story, "Maiden, Maiden," which he had read in 1950 and which not only had a striking mountain background but a strong dramatic situation: a young woman, emotionally involved with two men, waiting in a hut for them to return from a mountain climb and learning that there has been an accident and only one of them is coming back. Which one? And which one does she want?

This basic idea was then worked on and elaborated by the writer Michael Austin, who had previously scripted *The Shout* (based on a Robert Graves short story) for Jerzy Skolimowski. Austin had two particular gifts that Zinnemann could utilize for this project: a love of the outdoors, which would sharpen his research into the mountaineering aspects of the story; and the ability to write very sparse, elliptical dialogue that could suggest tensions and implications beneath the ostensible meanings of the words. For Zinnemann it was to be a drama that "reads between the lines." Austin manages this remarkably well, particularly in his depiction of secretly guilty people inspecting innocuous queries for lethal implications. Even a comic line of awkward communication to explain why transport for Douglas (Sean Connery) and Kate (Betsy Brantley) is late—"The bus has lost a shoe"—reverberates later: the discovery of a "lost shoe" is to have a momentous effect in the narrative.

Two major changes were made to the original story. Although the story was set in 1932 and the period is kept that way in the film (Zinnemann wanted to convey the silence and purity of the mountains before the advent of modern tourism), both director and writer felt that adultery was not a strong enough explanation to convey the necessary guilt, inhibition and obsession of the relationship between Douglas and Kate. After all, what is so special about a "dirty weekend" and why couldn't the doctor simply divorce his wife and live with the girl? Austin's solution was to make the relationship one between uncle and niece. He does not give this too much weight (the film is not about incest in any meaningful way), but that relationship does provide a barrier, an emotional block that the characters have some difficulty in breaking through.

There is a second major addition to the story. Zinnemann wished to integrate into the narrative one of the elements of mountaineering folklore: that people who had fallen into a glacier crevasse and whose bodies had never been recovered sometimes turned up 30 or 40 years later, usually unrecognizable, but on rare occasions with their features miraculously preserved in ice. This addition leads to the finest scene in the film and indeed lifts the film onto a different plane of myth and poetry. On one of their

Six—Maidens and Mountains

climbing expeditions, Douglas slips in attempting to jump across a crevasse and drops his axe. In going to retrieve it, the guide Johann (Lambert Wilson) comes across a shoe sticking out of the ice. The brother of Johann's grandfather had disappeared many years ago on the eve of his wedding. The body is dug out and the identity confirmed. The man's fiancée, who has never married, is brought to the glacier. The very old peasant woman looks at her young man, almost perfectly preserved in the ice—and looking uncannily like Johann.

The weight given to this discovery is significant not only because it portends a death to come. In some ways, it contains the thematic weight of the film: time, youth and age. An aged spinster in black confronts her dead lover whose youth has been preserved while she has withered in his absence. It is as she has always seen him in her memory and a poignant image of the way time has stood still for her after his death, a life frozen in frustration. The old lady's experience anticipates the fate of Kate, who at the end is also devastated by the loss of the youth she has loved—and perhaps, by the loss of her own youth.

Loss of innocence is a key theme in the film. It justifies the emphasis given to the fall and explains why it is the young man who has to die. It is thematically vital that the mountain is called the Maiden, with two distinct faces to the men, like Kate herself, and whom both men, young and old, make an unavailing attempt to scale. (The point would have been clearer if the film had kept to its original title, "Maiden, Maiden," which makes its reference to both the mountain and the girl quite clear. Zinnemann's yielding to front-office pressure about the change of title became one of the things about the film he most regretted.) This theme of innocence also gives a different inflection to the setting of the film in 1932, which was a more innocent time, when people could still be shocked by an illicit or unconventional sexual relationship (the reaction of the hotel when they think Douglas and Kate *are* married is stilted enough) and before a European holocaust would obliterate forever any doubts about the darker recesses of the human soul.

In an interview in *The Times* (October 20, 1982), Sean Connery perceptively likened Douglas to an Ibsen character, "ostensibly a pillar of the community, but ruled by his darker emotions." He plays the part with a similar mastery of understanding (and Zinnemann said that he never at any stage considered anybody other than Connery for that role). The events leading up to Douglas's affair with Kate are flashback revelations that puncture the present narrative and cast a pall of passion and apprehension over it. The love scene between them in the deserted house (when his wife Sarah and Kate's mother have gone on an excursion) is ingeniously split into two. When Douglas recalls it, he is sheltering from a storm with Kate and Johann. The thunder rolling overhead seems to connect with the passion he felt as he ascended the dark stairs, and his flashback ends as he approaches Kate in the room, the memory enfolded within a storm that has now passed over. But for Kate, it now seems less romantic, more ominous. What she recalls in her flashback of the event is not only the passionate embrace, but the moment when Douglas's wife knocks on the door and almost finds them there.

The whole scene is beautifully done. When they embrace, the passion between them is conveyed by the sight and sound of Kate's beads hitting the floor. On the one hand, this is sexually suggestive and yet visually inexplicit in the exemplary manner of classical cinema. But it also relates back to the moment when Kate in her office has been waiting for the return of Douglas after ten years and has been standing at the window chewing her necklace in frustration. The love scene is the moment when this chain of frustration, which has formed around Kate's whole life, has finally been broken. Above all, the image of the beads tumbling onto the floor is an eerie premonition of the latter rock fall that is to send the lives of the three main characters tumbling into confusion.

Sarah's interruption compels Douglas to hide in a dark corner behind the door (in direct contrast to the Alpine scenery, which gives Douglas a temporary release, a feeling that his emotional life as well as his physical life can be lived out in the open). To arrive at Kate's door, Sarah has had to walk along a dark corridor, the sound of a single bead hitting the dressing table sending the tiniest sliver of suspicion down her spine and giving a momentary hint of the unknown and the fear that is rooted deep in her subconscious. Later in the film, the moment is to be recalled when Johann

Sean Connery as the doctor who falls in love with his niece, Kate (Betsy Brantley), in *Five Days One Summer*, a Ladd Company Production/Warner Bros., 1982.

knocks at Kate's door in the hotel after approaching it down a dark corridor, and is made aware that Kate and Douglas have just made love through Kate's almost involuntary gesture of opening the door wider so that he can see. This again links back to the first love scene between Douglas and Kate. Running to her room in a flurry ambiguously poised between invitation and escape, Kate nevertheless leaves the door open, neither abetting nor resisting the situation, seeming to lay a trap which the men are quite visibly to fall into.

For Kate, the affair with Douglas is a dream from which she much waken. For Douglas, it is a re-kindling of youth. It is another dimension of that scene between the old lady and her dead lover. The stark contrast between youth and age evokes Douglas' relationship with Kate. It is this which fuels Johann's accusation against Douglas when he discovers the truth about the two of them. He is a thief, claims Johann, and is stealing Kate's youth from her; and how can she give herself to an old man who does not even belong to her? For Douglas, the dead young man in the snow is implicitly an idealized image of himself: of youth preserved. His relationship with Kate is an attempt on his part to cheat time, to arrest the onset of middle age. The imagery comments poignantly on both the inevitability of the aging process and the desperate attempts to check this erosion (like Douglas' early gesture in the hotel room of tossing the rope over the Swiss clock to stop it from ticking: the gesture of a mature man in love attempting to make time stand still).

As the film develops, the tension on Douglas grows. He looks at the Maiden and says, "*That's* what I came for," and momentarily he could be speaking about the maiden (Kate) or the mountain. Both are calls to his youth; both are eventually to reject him. The mountaineering aspect of the film becomes a metaphor for the relationships. The shot of a frayed length of rope stretching at a moment of danger late in the film seems to suggest a *mind* at the end of its tether. Characters pull at and are tied to each other, and are afraid of letting go. In some ways, the whole film is about "letting go": Douglas's refusal to let Kate go; Johann's insistence that Kate should let Douglas go; the "letting go" of the deep bank of suppressed emotions (like the glacier, the repressions have been melting year by year); Sarah's clinging to her marriage and to the ties that bind (the last time we see her she is fastening Douglas' bow-tie for him). Everything gathers towards that moment when the young man can no longer hold onto his precarious grip on the Maiden—and chaos descends on them all.

When the Maiden has been first glimpsed, Johann has commented: "She doesn't look too difficult from here. But you'll be surprised when you see her from the other side." Even in its context, the remark seems to have a deeper meaning, extending to the complex tangled emotions of the characters beneath the surface of polite, civilized exteriors. In its overall application to the film, the remark has quite profound implications on several levels.

Although its relatively small cast and slim storyline might suggest a fairly straightforward film to make, *Five Days One Summer* did encounter a number of difficulties not visible, as it were, from the other side. It was physically an arduous film to shoot, requiring the help of mountaineer and documentary filmmaker Norman Dyhrenfurth, director of the second unit, and careful tutelage in the art of climbing for cast and crew by the famous experts Hamish MacInnes and Joe Brown. Because of the location shooting, everyone in the crew had to practice being winched up by helicopter, because if the weather had turned bad, this would have been the only way off. Because of the danger, a doctor was on hand throughout the shooting, although, in fact, only one minor accident occurred. Another formidable task, brilliantly achieved in the film by Zinnemann's usual designer Willy Holt, was the construction of a hotel at which Douglas and Kate stay. It was so convincing that Zinnemann was asked afterwards where reservations could be made!

Another risky side of the venture was the casting of two unknowns in the roles of Kate and Johann. Betsy Brantley was discovered in the chorus of *The Best Little Whorehouse in Texas* at Drury Lane, and brings great sensitivity to the capricious and independent moods of Kate. Zinnemann remembered Lambert Wilson from a small but important role he had played in *Julia*, as the man who delivers the hatbox to Lillian on the train. Because his English was so good, Wilson (son of the eminent French actor, Georges Wilson) could concentrate on the nuances of his character and on eliciting Johann's odd provincial puritanism. (Johann is the moralist of the film, which might be another reason why he is the most vulnerable.) One should also mention Jennifer Hilary's fine performance as Douglas' wife, Sarah, concealing a reservoir of pain beneath the proprieties of restraint. With such an interesting cast and with an offbeat narrative, the film's commercial prospects seemed promising. Yet a sign that the film might not immediately find its audience came with disappointing previews in America. After these previews, the symphonic score of Carl Davis was replaced with an intimate one by Elmer Bernstein, which takes its scale more from the people than the settings. But the film's critical and commercial performance in England was also rather disappointing, and it might be worthwhile considering the reasons.

Like the Maiden, the film looks simple but has hidden depths, and these depths were not perceived. Nearly every critic mentioned it as a Zinnemann film and attempted to relate it to his preceding work. One can recognize the customary technical finish and the outstanding photographic quality, Giuseppe Rotunno's camerawork making of the film a visual Alpine Symphony that not only responds to the grandeur of the setting but creates of it a character in its own right. But, in some ways, the most striking thing about *Five Days One Summer* is its difference from the usual Zinnemann films. One wonders if the critical disappointment did not simply spring from the fact that it was not what they expected. The most characteristic Zinnemann films are about conscience, the awareness of right and wrong: *Five Days One Summer* is about obsession, the kind of feeling so overpowering that it sweeps aside social and moral laws. Other Zinnemann films are about standing fast: this one is about letting go.

Stylistically, too, the film is a departure for Zinnemann. Usually the style has been the servant of its subject, which is not to say that it is uninteresting or unoriginal, but that it does not draw immediate attention to itself. (As John Frankenheimer once said: "I think Fred Zinnemann has never let style bother him. And yet I would say that probably Fred Zinnemann knows more about the camera than any other director around.") But *Five Days One Summer* is unquestionably a director's film, in which one is as aware of the eye that is beholding these narrative events as the events themselves. Now, for many critics, the "cinema of directors" has lost its charm, submerged by the squabbles of auteurism. For most audiences it never meant much anyway: Few people went to see a film because of who directed it. The modern cinema is much more concerned with duplicating winning formulas and displaying technical gadgetry than encouraging personal expression. With its careful visual presentation, oblique narrative and enigmatic characterization, *Five Days One Summer* seemed too precious, too fragile to survive in the cinema of special effects. But, for Fred Zinnemann, it was a labour of love: a very private film which no-one else could have made and which, for anyone who has followed his career closely, has treasures to disclose. It has a peculiar hermetic beauty of a kind that often characterizes the later works of artists who have refined style and theme to an abstract purity of expression. At the time of their appearance, such works often seem obscure, forbidding, even impenetrable: a longer perspective forces a different perception.

The great Norwegian dramatist, Henrik Ibsen, once said: "It's the dramatist's function to ask questions, not to supply answers." Fred Zinnemann always subscribed to that. If there is one work of art that *Five Days One Summer* resembles more than any other, it is Ibsen's *When We Dead Awaken* (incidentally, a much better title for Zinnemann's film, which is also about the dead reawakening to claim the living). Both works have triangular relationships, particularly involving an older man and his young "wife"; both have a mountain setting and nebulous narratives that end with a fall from the heights. Both works are testaments of a kind from individualists who started in realism and moved in these works to a poetic symbolism. *Five Days One Summer* has a movement and complex inner music that feels closer to poetry than prose. Its dramatic force comes, unusually, not from character and a sense of claustrophobia but rather from its silences and a sense of space. The reunion between Kate and the survivor of the rockfall is filmed in imperious long shot in what Zinnemann called his "*Big Parade* ending": The emotional effect is muted but the visual patterning is remarkable. In a way, in *Five Days One Summer*, the mountain *is* Fred Zinnemann—impassively watching, holding the fate of the characters in his hands. In this film, in exploring the fissure between majestic Nature and frail human nature, he (to borrow a striking phrase from the book of *The Nun's Story*) "reached the icy peaks of total detachment."

Conclusion:
The Quiet Master

> Playing some of the scenes with Van Heflin, working with an artist like Zinnemann—after years of literally nothing—was a tonic. The way we worked, talking about it, thinking about it, using, discarding, trying something else. It was good. It was the way it ought to be—always.
> —Mary Astor, *A Life on Film*

> Working with him is a permanent lesson in integrity.
> —Peter Ustinov, *Dear Me*

In January 1996, approximately a year before the director's death, the prestigious British film periodical *Sight and Sound* published a glossy dossier on Fred Zinnemann as a supplement to its usual magazine. The exact provenance of this document was unexplained and mysterious, for it appeared not to represent any editorial preference or commitment: After all, *Sight and Sound* had not published an interview with, or article on, Zinnemann for 35 years. Nor did it seem to represent a change of heart for when, encouraged by the appearance of this dossier, I wrote to the editor and suggested an article on *Act of Violence* as a follow-up, I never even had the courtesy of a reply, let alone a refusal. (May I say that I have invariably found American editors much more considerate in this regard than their British counterparts.) A distinguished ex-editor of *Sight and Sound*, Penelope Houston, used to say Hollywood had Orson Welles on its conscience. I wondered if Fred Zinnemann was on someone's conscience, the dossier filling a perceived gap in appreciation. Certainly the lineup of Zinnemann's peers and fellow professionals offering tributes was an impressive one: Deborah Kerr, Robert Wise, Walter Murch, Vanessa Redgrave, Edward Fox, John Hurt, Paul Scofield, Peter Ustinov, and Douglas Slocombe, among others. What was conspicuously absent was a contribution from the critical fraternity.

In 1968, the guru of auteurism, Andrew Sarris, had published *The American Cinema*, his deeply personal, massively controversial classification of Hollywood directors, placing Zinnemann in his notorious "Less Than Meets The Eye" category. Actually Zinnemann was in good company (this category has always seemed to me as distinguished as Sarris' pantheon): It included such masters as Billy Wilder, William Wyler, Elia Kazan, David Lean, Joseph L. Mankiewicz and John Huston. One might have imagined that a director as honored by the industry and respected by his peers as Zinnemann would have regarded such critical polemicism with an amused detachment. In fact, and coming at about the time of the traumatic cancellation of *Man's Fate*, Sarris's judgement had, I believe, as damaging an effect on Zinnemann's self-confidence (which was never very secure) as François Truffaut's vitriolic attack did on the old masters of French cinema, such as Marcel Carné, René Clément and Henri-Georges Clouzot—or, for that matter, the later, notorious New York critics' attack on David Lean for *Ryan's Daughter*, which left him in a state of shock. Of course, Zinnemann continued to make good films in the 1970s; had his critical champions (most notably, Pauline Kael and Louis Giannetti in America); and the declared respect of the socially conscious, succeeding generation of directors such as Sidney Lumet, Martin Ritt and John Frankenheimer. But when Donald Spoto, in his 1978 critical biography of Stanley Kramer, referred to Zinnemann as a director "oddly neglected by both academic and cultists," he was not exaggerating, and the truth of that neglect, I believe, gnawed at Zinnemann.

In my early encounters with him, I was sometimes taken aback by what seemed his bitterness towards some individuals for not giving him his critical due or for trying to steal his artistic thunder. (These came as a surprise because, for the most part, our conversations were conducted with the utmost civility.) He would ask me to switch off my recording machine while he delivered his harsh opinions on Stanley Kramer, whom he thought an opportunist who had behaved dishonorably on *High Noon*, or on Elmo Williams, whom he accused of making his reputation on the fake claim that he had rescued *High Noon* in the cutting room. (When I talked to Kramer and Williams, they had no such harsh things to say about Zinnemann and were generous in their praise of his qualities as director.) Daniel Taradash told me that Zinnemann had fallen out with Carl Foreman over an article the latter had written for *The Observer* magazine about the Western, in which Foreman had cited *High Noon* without mentioning the director. I remembered the piece well, and, in the context of the article, there was no particular reason why the director should have been mentioned. Nevertheless, and despite a handsome apology by Foreman for this omission printed in the following week's issue, Zinnemann was deeply offended and their friendship was damaged as a result. In a similar vein, a friend at the National Film Theatre in London told me of an occasion when Zinnemann had taken exception to a negative note in the program booklet about *The Member of the Wedding* and had personally phoned the contributor to express his displeasure. I know from personal observation that he was wounded by his (admittedly unforgivable) omission in Richard Roud's 1980 two-volume round-up of major filmmakers, *Cinema: A Critical Dictionary*. He was as hypersensitive to being slighted as only a person can be whose surname begins with the last letter of the alphabet; and he had a right to feel aggrieved, even until the end. After all, in the interim, Wilder, Wyler, Huston, Lean have all had critical cudgels taken up on their behalf, whereas, comparatively speaking, Zinnemann has not. Given the respect and honor of his fellow professionals, should it have mattered to him? Maybe not, but it did. When Sarris seemed to be mellowing towards him in the early 1980s at the time of *Five Days One Summer*, Zinnemann had sent me a copy of his *Village Voice* review;

and I found it oddly touching to notice that Sarris' reference to what he called the "marvelously civilized" quality he had found in the film had been highlighted by Zinnemann in his yellow marker-pen.

I had first seen Zinnemann in person when he had appeared unexpectedly at a National Film Theatre tribute in London to his old friend William Wyler, who, judging from his surprise and delight when spotting Fred, seemed also not to know he was coming. A slightly built, reticent man, Zinnemann seemed to have stolen in unannounced and stood quietly in a corner until recognized rather than made a more assertive entrance. Later, when we worked together on an ultimately aborted authorized biography, I came to view him as a fascinating, outwardly friendly, quietly fearsome personality. In the early stages of our collaboration, we got on extremely well: it was only later that things became problematic. Looking back, I understand his concern. My inclinations were more towards critical appreciation than biography, and although he liked what I had written in that vein, I was not giving him what he wanted. Our collaboration ended when I discovered that another writer had been brought in without my being told or at that stage even being paid. (This may have been more the result of a series of misunderstandings rather than malice, though I was to learn that this was not the only occasion on which this kind of thing had happened.) However, I was pleased that eventually, and with substantial help from Alexander Walker, he was able to complete a book to his satisfaction, an autobiography replete with wonderful photographs and a personal account of his life that gives away next to nothing about the man. I had come to the conclusion that, as with Hitchcock, the private desires and frustrations of Zinnemann were actually displaced, sublimated and transferred into the films. "Behind that quiet courtesy," Stanley Kramer told me, "there's an iron rod"; and behind the taciturn integrity of Gary Cooper's Marshal in *High Noon* and the principled stubbornness of Prewitt in *From Here to Eternity* ("If a man don't go his own way, he's nothin'"), I see Fred Zinnemann.

I was a relatively inexperienced writer then, and the experience with Zinnemann left me a bit shaken. I did not fully grasp what had happened until I read with a shock of recognition that passage in William Goldman's classic account of screenwriting, *Adventures in the Screen Trade* (1984), where he talks of those directors who are "writer-killers." They ask you for apples, says Goldman, but when you give them apples, they say pomegranates would be preferable, but when you write pomegranates that does not satisfy them either. "And it goes on," says Goldman, "rewrite following rewrite, until your mind is fucked around. You are frustrated, confused, maybe useless." Goldman takes care to stress that he is, in some cases, talking about extremely good directors, some of whose best friends might be writers; but the experience for the writer is still demoralizing. Goldman's description conformed exactly to my experience with Zinnemann. I would write something that would meet with his complete approval one week and then next week appear to him deeply flawed; I would follow his instructions to the letter only for the work to be deemed unsatisfactory; I once made a literal transcription of something he told to me on tape only for the passage to be rejected because, in print, he said, it did not sound like him. At one stage, I was getting an average of three phone calls from him every ten minutes. I daresay this might be a quite normal screenwriting experience, and I have always had great sympathy for William Wyler's dictum that what counts in film is the end product not the suffering undergone to achieve it. ("They might hate me on the set, but they'll love me at the premiere," as he put it.) But it was not bringing out the best in me.

A symptom of this was the occasion when I had been commissioned to write the program notes for a 1982 Zinnemann season at the National Film Theatre in London. Ordinarily this would have caused me no qualms: It was a small project of a kind I had done effectively several times before, and should have taken no time at all. However, knowing that Zinnemann himself would be reading this and scrutinizing every line (and I do mean *every* line), I had the most severe case of writer's block I have suffered in over 20 years of writing, and eventually submitted what I still think is the worst thing I have ever had published, making him sound like a masochistic moralist with all the mass appeal of a Carl Dreyer or Robert Bresson. (Several years later, when I was given a similar commission to commemorate the publication of his autobiography,

I had no such problems but, by that time, I had not been in contact with Zinnemann for a long time.) After a particularly fraught period of misunderstanding, non-communication and monumental crossing of wires, I felt compelled to issue an ultimatum: I will deliver a manuscript by Christmas, but only if I am left completely alone, and incommunicado, for the next six weeks. This was agreed and honored. Surmounting a massive psychological block that had built around me at this time concerning anything to do with Zinnemann (I could not even write his name and it was several years before I could bring myself to watch a film of his again), I drafted a complete manuscript. I do remember referring to it as "Pandora's Box" when I delivered it to him personally at his offices in Mayfair just before Christmas. On Boxing Day, he rang me to say he was delighted with it, but obviously had many suggestions to make. Over the next three months or so, we worked over the text, discussing all his suggested improvements, omissions, reformulations and such, which were then incorporated into a final typed version. (The text published now is essentially that text which Zinnemann endorsed, the major exception being the placing of the chapter on *A Hatful of Rain*, which he wanted in the "Aftermath of War" section and which I always felt fitted better under "Variations on a Theme.") I left the manuscript with him, to do with as he saw fit. It was only when the Berlin Film Festival expressed an interest in seeing and then publishing it that I learned that another writer had been brought in and was working on a new version.

How typical my experience was is difficult to say. I was later to find that other writers had had similar experiences with him, including one who told me he had been reduced to a state of near-suicidal despair when he had discovered by chance that Zinnemann, out of dissatisfaction with his work (which he had never directly expressed to the writer), had brought in another writer to re-work the material. In fairness, I must also record that other writers who contacted me, such as Robert Anderson (*The Nun's Story*), and Jon Cleary (*The Sundowners*), were full of praise for Zinnemann's insights, support and professionalism.

My relations with him during our collaboration were always cordial without being closely personal. All the interviews were conducted in his office, which I remember as a bare, austere room, illuminated by a single lamp, and reminding me a bit of the torture room in *The Day of the Jackal*. I do not know whether others found him difficult to work for, though I did notice that he had at least three different secretaries during the short time I was dealing with him. We never went for a meal together nor was I ever offered anything stronger to drink that mineral water: not a lack of hospitality, I am sure, but a reflection of what I surmised was the formality of the relationship, as he saw it, and austerity of Zinnemann's own personality, which I always felt fed into his films. (David Shipman had once said to me that, greatly as he admired Zinnemann's films, he always thought they were too "finished," had been given that one extra polish that took a little life, vitality and spontaneity out of them. I felt this too and it might explain my fondness for *Teresa* which seems to get slightly out of his control and consequently has a warmth and very human messiness that is absent elsewhere from this most fastidious of filmmakers.) At the same time, he was never less than courteous and thoughtful, for example, sending a delightful telegram to my wife and myself on the birth of our first child that congratulated the child on her choice of parents: That was typical of his quietly ironical humor. When I researched into other filmmakers, I never found one who did not speak of Zinnemann with enormous affection and respect, particularly younger directors appreciative of his encouragement—like Jack Clayton, who was overwhelmed to be invited to lunch by Zinnemann after the latter had seen and admired Clayton's debut feature, *Room at the Top*.

What was his secret? The impression he gave was of a man of iron will and self-discipline, a temperament ameliorated sometimes by a saucy sense of fun. It would need the biographical skills of a Patrick McGilligan to penetrate the surface of Zinnemann's calm and dig into what I suspect was a morass of complexity, repression and retentiveness. What must he have felt, for example, during the period when he was safe in America while his parents were imperilled in Europe? Listening to him once on the radio on the BBC's *Desert Island Discs* program, where he chose his favourite pieces of music—a predictable mixture of Bach, Brahms, Beethoven, and Mahler—I was enthralled by the attempt of the interviewer, Sue Lawley, to prize out of a clearly discomfited

Zinnemann some information about the fate of his parents: Could he have got them out of Europe to America before they perished in a concentration camp? He would not elaborate, and it is inevitable to speculate that he might understandably have felt great guilt about being unable to save them from the European nightmare. It is significant, though, that the films which first drew him to public and critical attention were both war subjects: *The Seventh Cross*, which challenged Nazi stereotypes and offered a compassionate picture of a pre-war German society in the grip of a great evil (it might also be seen as his defense of the controversial decision to stay in Germany of his great idol, the conductor Wilhelm Furtwängler); and *The Search*, the harrowing but eventual hopeful evocation of post-war Europe and its reparation from the ruins. It would confirm my view that Zinnemann expressed himself most deeply not in his life but in his films. This might be another reason that he was so sensitive to their being undervalued.

Like Hitchcock, like David Lean, Zinnemann had seemed content to be seen as a craftsman until relatively late in his career, when he suddenly became more insistent on being recognized as an "artist." See, for example, his interview with Jack Kroll in *Newsweek* (22 November, 1982), where he was quoted as expressing annoyance at the word "craftsman" and asserting that his instincts were those of an artist. (Hitchcock similarly upbraided an interviewer for referring to his mastery of the "tricks of the trade": wouldn't "technique" be a better word?) Twenty years on, it seems to me that Zinnemann's claim of artistry has been vindicated. The reputation of *High Noon* might have temporarily slumped when cult favorite Howard Hawks took his pseudo-macho side-swipe at it in talking of *Rio Bravo*; but, half a century on, it still looks an irreducible classic and one of the best Westerns ever made (for voters at the National Film Theatre in a poll taken some years ago, *the* best Western ever made). For all Philip French's description of it as the time as "the thinking man's *Sound of Music*," Zinnemann's *Man for All Seasons* still sets the standard for thoughtful, popular historical costume drama. Remakes of it, and of *The Member of the Wedding* and *Day of the Jackal*, only have the effect of making one pine for the Zinnemann original.

For all its hi-tech special effects, a modern blockbuster like *Pearl Harbor* (2001) only summons up nostalgia for the infinitely more involving human drama of *From Here to Eternity* and for the absence of a Zinnemann equivalent in modern cinema.

Zinnemann had his fair share of career disappointments and unrealized projects. He talks about some of these in his autobiography and the fate of mouth-watering projects like *Hawaii* and *Custer* (with Toshiro Mifune as Crazy Horse!) that never came to fruition in his hands have been finely dealt with elsewhere by, respectively, Paul Mayersberg and Wendell Mayes (see bibliography). His achievement remains considerable, however. He was a much loved figure in the industry. When shooting had finished on *A Man for All Seasons* and he asked the company how they should celebrate, Dame Wendy Hiller said she spoke for them all when she replied: "Nothing would be nicer than to go on shooting." Said Lord Richard Attenborough: "I have never been disappointed by a Fred Zinnemann picture."

His was a humane cinema. He was a noble, independent voice in an industry tending to conformity, whose films of conscience communicated with mass audiences without ever condescending to them. For people of my film-loving generation, who were growing up as the sun was setting on the Hollywood studio empire, he was one of those giants (like William Wyler, Billy Wilder, George Stevens, and John Huston) whose films gave you an exciting time but also made you think; who demonstrated that films could entertain but could also—in the best sense of the word—educate. I have come to treasure the intelligent question marks of his endings, the deep decency of his vision. With this book, I hope I have gone some way towards rectifying a critical omission and injustice; and laid a troubled ghost to rest.

Filmography

AS ASSISTANT CAMERAMAN

La Marche des Machines (France, 1927: Dir. Eugene Deslaw)
Ich Kusse Ihre Hand, Madame (Germany, 1929: Dir. Robert Land)
Sprengbagger 1010 (Germany, 1929: Dir. Karl Ludwig Achaz-Duiberg)
Menschen am Sonntag (Germany, 1929: Dir. Robert Siodmak)

AS FILM EXTRA

All Quiet on the Western Front (USA, 1930: Dir. Lewis Milestone)

AS ASSISTANT TO DIRECTOR BERTHOLD VIERTEL

Man Trouble (USA, 1931: Starring Dorothy Mackaill, Milton Sills)
The Spy (USA, 1931: Starring Kay Johnson, Neil Hamilton)
The Wiser Sex (USA, 1932: Starring Claudette Colbert, Clive Brook)
Also assisted Busby Berkeley and Gregg Toland on the dance sequences in *The Kid from Spain* (USA, 1932: Dir. Leo McCarey, starring Eddie Cantor); and acted as technical adviser to William

Wyler on the Vienna sequence in *These Three* (USA, 1936: Starring Merle Oberon, Miriam Hopkins)

AS DOCUMENTARY DIRECTOR

The Wave (1934) Screenplay: Henwar Rodakiewicz. Photography: Paul Strand. Editing: Gunther von Fritsch. Music: Sylvestre Revueltas. Producer: Paul Strand, Mexican Department of Fine Arts. 60 mins.

Benjy (1951) Screenplay: Stewart Stern. Photography: J. Peverell Marley. Editing: George Tomasini. Players: Lee Aaker, Neville Brand. Production Orthopaedic Foundation of Los Angeles/Paramount. 30 mins.

Oscar for Best Documentary (Short Subjects)

SHORTS DIRECTED (all for MGM)

Friend Indeed (1937) A Pete Smith Specialty. One reel.

The Story of Dr. Carver (1937) Starring Clinton Rosemond. A Pete Smith Specialty. One reel.

That Mothers Might Live (1938) Narration: John Nesbitt. Starring Shepperd Strudwick. One reel.

Oscar for Best Short Film (one reel).

Tracking the Sleeping Death (1938) Narration Carey Wilson. One reel.

They Live Again (1938) Narration: John Nesbitt. One reel.

Weather Wizards (1939) "Crime Does Not Pay" Series. Two reels.

Help Wanted! (1939) "Crime Does Not Pay" Series. Two reels.

One Against the World (1939) Starring Jonathan Hale. "John Nesbitt's Passing Parade Series." One reel.

The Ash-Can Fleet (1939) One reel.

Forgotten Victory (1939) "John Nesbitt's Passing Parade" Series. One reel.

The Old South (1940) One reel.

Stuffie (1940) Narration Pete Smith. A Pete Smith Specialty. One reel.

A Way in the Wilderness (1940) Starring Shepperd Strudwick. "John Nesbitt's Passing Parade" Series. One reel.

The Great Meddler (1940) A Carey Wilson Miniature. One reel.

Forbidden Passage (1941) "Crime Does Not Pay" Series. Two reels. Oscar Nomination for Best Short Film (two-reel).
Your Last Act (1941) "John Nesbitt's Passing Parade" Series. One reel.
The Lady or the Tiger? (1942) A Carey Wilson Miniature. One reel.

FEATURES DIRECTED

Kid Glove Killer (1942) Screenplay: Allen Rivkin, John C. Higgins (story by John C. Higgins). Photography: Paul Vogel. Editing: Ralph Winters. Music: David Snell. Leading Players: Van Heflin (Gordan McKay), Marsha Hunt (Jane Mitchell), Lee Bowman (Gerry Latimer). Producer: Jack Chertok. MGM. 74 mins.

Eyes in the Night (1942) Screenplay: Guy Trosper, Howard Emmett Rogers (from the novel "Odour of Violets" by Bayard Kendrick). Photography: Robert Planck, Charles Lawton. Editing: Ralph Winters. Music: Lennie Hayton. Leading Players: Edward Arnold (Duncan MacLain), Ann Harding (Normal Lawry), Donna Reid (Barbara Lawry), "Friday" (Alsation). Producer: Jack Chertok. MGM. 79 mins.

The Seventh Cross (1944) Screenplay: Helen Deutsch (from the novel by Anna Seghers). Photography: Karl Freund. Art Director: Cedric Gibbons, Leonid Vasian. Editing: Thomas Richards. Music: Roy Webb. Leading Players: Spencer Tracy (George Heisler), Signe Hasso (Toni), Hume Cronyn (Paul Roeder), Jessica Tandy (Liasel Roeder), Agnes Moorehead (Madame Marelli). Producer: Pandro S. Berman. MGM. 112 mins. Oscar Nomination for Hume Cronyn (Best Supporting Actor).

Little Mister Jim (1946) Screenplay: George Bruce (from the novel "Army Brat" by Tommy Wadelton). Photography: Lester White. Art Direction: Cedric Gibbons, Hubert Hobson. Editing: Frank Hull. Music: George Bassman. Leading Players: "Butch" Jenkins (Little Jim Tucker), James Craig (Big Jim Tucker), Chingwah Lee (Sui Jen). Producer: Orville O. Dull. MGM. 92 mins.

My Brother Talks to Horses (1947) Screenplay: Morton Thompson (from his story, "Lewie, My Brother Who Talks to Horses"). Photography: Harold Rosson. Art Direction: Cedric Gibbons, Leonid Vasian. Editing: George White. Music: Rudolph G. Kopp. Leading Players: Peter Lawford (John Penrose), "Butch" Jenkins

(Lewie Penrose), Beverly Tyler (Martha), Edward Arnold (Mr Bledsoe), Spring Byington (Mrs Penrose). Producer: Samuel Marx. MGM. 93 mins.

The Search (1948) Screenplay: Richard Schweizer, David Wechsler (additional dialogue by Paul Jarrico). Photography: Emil Berna. Editing: Herman Haller. Music: Robert Blum. Leading Players: Montgomery Clift (Ralph Stevenson), Ivan Jandl (the boy), Aline MacMahon (Mrs Malik). Producer: Lazar Wechsler. For Praessens Film-Swiss and MGM release. 105 mins. Oscar for Richard Schweizer and David Wechsler (Best Motion Picture Story) and special miniature statuette for Ivan Jandl for outstanding juvenile performance. Oscar Nomination for Montgomery Clift (Best Actor), Fred Zinnemann (Best Director), Richard Schweizer and David Wechsler (Best Screenplay).

Act of Violence (1949) Screenplay: Robert L. Richards (Story by Collier Young). Photography: Robert Surtees. Art Direction: Cedric Gibbons, Hans Peters. Editing: Conrad A. Nervig. Music: Bronislau Kaper. Leading Players: Van Heflin (Frank Enley), Robert Ryan (Joe Parkson), Janet Leigh (Edith Enley), Mary Astor (Pat), Phyllis Thaxter (Ann), Barry Kroeger (Johnny). Producer: William H. Wright. MGM. 82 mins.

The Men (1950) Screenplay: Carl Foreman. Photography: Robert de Grasse. Art Direction: Edward Boyle. Editing: Harry Gerstad. Music: Dimitri Tiomkin. Leading Players: Marlon Brando (Ken Wilozek), Teresa Wright (Ellen), Everett Sloane (Dr. Brock), Jack Webb (Norm), Richard Erdman (Leo). Producer: Stanley Kramer. United Artists. 85 mins. Oscar Nomination for Carl Foreman (Story and Screenplay).

Teresa (1951) Screenplay: Stewart Stern (story by Alfred Hayes, Stewart Stern). Photography: William J. Miller. Art Direction: Leo Kerz. Editing: Frank Sullivan. Music: Louis Appelbaum. Leading Players: Pier Angeli (Teresa), John Ericson (Philip Cass), Patricia Collinge (Mother), Richard Bishop (Father), Peggy Ann Garner (Susan), Ralph Meeker (Sgt. Dobbs). Producer: Arthur M. Loew. MGM. 105 mins. Oscar Nomination for Alfred Hayes and Stewart Stern (Motion Picture Story).

High Noon (1952) Screenplay: Carl Foreman (from John W. Cunningham's story "The Tin Star"). Photography: Floyd Crosby. Art Direction: Rudolph Sternad, Ben Hayne. Editing: Elmo Williams, Harry Gerstad. Music: Dimitri Tiomkin. Leading Players: Gary

Cooper (Will Kane), Thomas Mitchell (Jonas Henderson), Lloyd Bridges (Harvey Pell), Katy Jurado (Helen Ramirez), Grace Kelly (Amy). Producer: Stanley Kramer. United Artists. 85 mins. Oscars for Gary Cooper (Best Actor) Elmo Williams and Harry Gerstad (Best Editing:), Dimitri Tiomkin (Best Score), Dimitri Tiomkin and Ned Washington (Best Song). Oscar Nominations for Best Film, Fred Zinnemann (Best Direction), Carl Foreman (Best Screenplay). New York Critics' Citation for Best Film and Best Direction.

The Member of the Wedding (1953) Screenplay: Edward and Edna Anhalt (from the play by Carson McCullers). Photography: Hal Mohr. Art Direction: Cary Odell. Editing: William Lyon. Music: Alex North. Leading Players: Julie Harris (Frankie Adams), Ethel Waters (Berenice), Brandon De Wilde (John Henry). Producer: Stanley Kramer. Columbia. 91 mins. Oscar Nomination for Julie Harris (Best Actress).

From Here to Eternity (1953) Screenplay: Daniel Taradash (from the novel by James Jones). Photography: Burnett Guffey. Art Direction: Cary Odell. Editing: William Lyon. Music: George Duning. Leading Players: Burt Lancaster (Sgt. Warden), Montgomery Clift (Robert E. Lee Prewitt), Deborah Kerr (Karen Holmes), Frank Sinatra (Angelo Maggio), Donna Reed (Lorene), Ernest Borgnine ("Fatso" Judson). Producer: Buddy Adler. Columbia. 118 mins. Oscars for Best Film, Frank Sinatra (Best Supporting Actor), Donna Reed (Best Supporting Actress), Fred Zinnemann (Best Direction), Daniel Taradash (Best Screenplay), Burnett Guffey (Best Black and White Photography), John Livadary (Best Sound), William Lyon (Best Editing). Oscar Nominations for Montgomery Clift (Best Actor), Burt Lancaster (Best Actor), Deborah Kerr (Best Actress), George Duning (Best Music). New York Film Critics' Citations for Best Film, Best Actor (Burt Lancaster), Best Direction. Directors Guild of America Award: Fred Zinnemann.

Oklahoma! (1955) Screenplay: Sonya Levien, William Ludwig (from the musical by Richard Rodgers and Oscar Hammerstein). Photography: Robert Surtees. Art Direction: Oliver Smith. Editing: Gene Ruggiero, George Boemler. Leading Players: Gordon MacRae (Curly), Shirley Jones (Laurey), Gloria Grahame (Ado Annie), Gene Nelson (Will Parker), Rod Steiger (Jud). Producer: Arthur Hornblow, Jr. Magna-RKO. 145 mins. Color/Todd A O.

Oscars for Fred Hynes (Best Sound), Robert Russell, Jay Blackton and Adolph Deutsch (Best Musical Scoring). Oscar Nominations for Robert Surtes (Best Color Photography:), Gene Ruggiero and George Boemler (Best Editing).

A Hatful of Rain (1957) Screenplay: Michael Vincent Gazzo, Alfred Hayes (from the play by Gazzo). Photography: Joe MacDonald. Art Direction: Lyle Wheeler, Leland Fuller. Editing: Dorothy Spencer. Music: Bernard Herrmann. Leading Players: Eva Marie Saint (Celia Pope), Don Murray (Johnny Pope), Anthony Franciosa (Polo), Lloyd Nolan (John Pope), Henry Silva ("Mother"). Producer: Buddy Adler. 20th Century–Fox. 109 mins. CinemaScope. Oscar Nomination for Anthony Franciosa (Best Actor). International Film Critics Award and Award for Best Actor (Anthony Franciosa) at 1957 Venice Film Festival.

The Nun's Story (1959) Screenplay: Robert Anderson (from the book by Kathryn C. Hulme). Photography: Franz Planer. Art Direction: Alexander Trauner. Editing: Walter Thompson. Music: Franz Waxman. Leading Players: Audrey Hepburn (Sister Luke), Peter Finch (Dr. Fortunati), Edith Evans (Mother Emmanuel), Peggy Ashcroft (Mother Mathilide), Dean Jagger (Dr. Van Der Mal), Mildred Dunnock (Sister Margharita). Producer: Henry Blanke. Warner Bros. 152 mins. Color. Oscar Nominations for Best Film, Audrey Hepburn (Best Actress), Fred Zinnemann (Best Director), Robert Anderson (Best Screenplay Adaptation), Franz Planer (Best Color Photography), George Groves (Best Sound), Walter Thompson (Best Editing), Franz Waxman (Best Score). New York Film Critics' Citations for Audrey Hepburn for Best Actress, and Fred Zinnemann (Best Direction). British Film Academy Award for Best British Actress (Audrey Hepburn).

The Sundowners (1960) Screenplay: Isobel Lennart, Jon Cleary (uncredited) (from the novel by Cleary). Photography: Jack Hildyard. Art Direction: Michael Stringer. Editing: Jack Harris. Music: Dimitri Tiomkin. Leading Players: Robert Mitchum (Paddy Carmody), Deborah Kerr (Ida Carmody), Peter Ustinov (Venneker), Glynis Johns (Mrs Firth), Dina Merill (Jean Halstead), Michael Anderson Jr. (Sean Carmody). Producer: Fred Zinnemann. Warner Bros. 124 mins. Color. Oscar Nominations for Best Film, Deborah Kerr (Best Actress), Glynis Johns (Best Supporting Actress), Fred Zinnemann (Best Director), Isobel

Lennart (Best Screenplay Adaptation). New York Film Critics' Citation for Best Actress (Deborah Kerr). National Board of Review Award for Robert Mitchum (Best Actor).

Behold a Pale Horse (1964) Screenplay: J.P. Miller (from the novel "Killing a Mouse on Sunday" by Emeric Pressburger). Photography: Jean Badal. Art Direction: Alexander Trauner, Auguste Capelier. Editing: Walter Thompson. Music: Maurice Jarre. Leading Players: Gregory Peck (Manuel Artiguez), Anthony Quinn (Cpt. Vinolas), Omar Sharif (Father Francisco), Raymond Pellegrin (Carlos), Marietto Angeletti (Paco). Producer: Fred Zinnemann. Highland-Brentwood/Columbia. 121 mins.

A Man for All Seasons (1966) Screenplay: Robert Bolt (from his own play). Photography: Ted Moore. Art Direction: John Box, Terence Marsh. Editing: Ralph Kemplen. Music: Georges Delerue. Leading Players: Paul Scofield (Thomas More), Wendy Hiller (Alice), Leo McKern (Cromwell), Robert Shaw (Henry VIII), Orson Welles (Cardinal Wolsey), Susannah York (Margaret), John Hurt (Richard Rich), Vanessa Redgrave (Anne Boleyn). Producer: Fred Zinnemann. Highland/Columbia. 120 mins. Oscars for Best Film, Paul Scofield (Best Actor), Fred Zinnemann (Best Direction), Robert Bolt (Best Screenplay Adaptation), Ted Moore (Best Color Photography), Elizabeth Haffenden and Joan Bridge (Best Color Costume Design). Oscar Nominations for Robert Shaw (Best Supporting Actor), Wendy Hiller (Best Supporting Actress). New York Film Critics' Citations for Best Film, Best Actor (Paul Scofield), Best Direction (Fred Zinnemann), Best Screenplay: (Robert Bolt). British Film Academy Awards for Best Film, Best British Film, Best British Actor (Paul Scofield), Best Screenplay (Robert Bolt), Best Color Photography (Ted Moore), Best Art Direction (John Box), Best Costume Design (Elizabeth Haffenden, Joan Bridge). Directors Guild Award: Fred Zinnemann.

The Day of the Jackal (1973) Screenplay: Kenneth Ross (from the novel by Frederick Forsyth). Photography: Jean Tournier. Art Direction: Willy Holt. Editing: Ralph Kemplen. Music: Georges Delerue. Leading Players: Edward Fox (The Jackal), Michel Lonsdale (Lebel), Eric Porter (Rodin), Delphine Seyrig (Colette), Alan Badel (the Minister), Donald Sinden (Mallinson), Cyril Cusack (Gozzi). Producer: John Woolf. Warwick/Universal. 142 mins. Color. Oscar Nomination for Ralph Kemplen (Best Editing).

British Film Academy Award for Best Film Editing (Ralph Kemplen).

Julia (1977) Screenplay: Alvin Sargent (from "Pentimento" by Lillian Hellman). Photography: Doulgas Slocombe. Art Direction: Gene Callahan, Willy Holt, Carmen Dillon. Editing: Walter Murch, Marcel Durham. Music: Georges Delerue. Leading Players: Jane Fonda (Lillian), Vanessa Redgrave (Julia), Jason Robards (Dashiell Hammett), Maximilian Schell (Johann), Meryl Streep (Anne Marie). Producer: Richard Roth. 20th Century–Fox. 117 mins. Color. Oscars for Jason Robards (Best Supporting Actor), Vanessa Redgrave (Best Supporting Actress), Alvin Sargent (Best Screenplay: Adaptation). Oscar Nominations for Best Film, Jane Fonda (Best Actress), Maximilian Schell (Best Supporting Actor), Fred Zinnemann (Best Direction), Douglas Slocombe (Best Photography), Walter Murch and Marcel Durham (Best Editing), Georges Delerue (Best Music Score), Anthea Sylbert (Best Costume Design). New York Film Critics' Citation for Best Supporting Actor (Maximilian Schell). British Film Academy Awards for Best Film, Best Actress (Jane Fonda), Best Screenplay (Alvin Sargent), Best Photography (Douglas Slocombe).

Five Days One Summer (1982) Screenplay: Michael Austin (based on the short story "Maiden, Maiden" by Kay Boyle). Photography: Giuseppe Rotunno. Art Direction: Willy Holt. Editing: Stuart Baird. Music: Elmer Bernstein. Leading Players: Sean Connery (Douglas), Betsy Brantley (Kate), Lambert Wilson (Johann), Jennifer Hilary (Sarah), Isabel Dean (Kate's Mother), Gerard Buhr (Brendel), Anna Massey (Jennifer Pierce), Sheila Reid (Gillian Pierce). Producer: Fred Zinnemann. Columbia-EMI-Warner. 108 mins. Color.

Appendix: Awards

Oscars

1938 *That Mothers Might Live* (Best One-Reel Short)
1951 *Benjy* (Best Short Documentary)
1953 *From Here to Eternity* (Best Director)
1966 *A Man for All Seasons* (Best Director)
1966 *A Man for All Seasons* (Best Picture)

Academy Award Nominations

1948 *The Search* (Director)
1952 *High Noon* (Director)
1959 *The Nun's Story* (Director)
1960 *The Sundowners* (Director)
1960 *The Sundowners* (Producer)
1977 *Julia* (Best Director)

New York Critics Awards

1952 *High Noon* (Director)
1953 *From Here to Eternity* (Director)

1959 *The Nun's Story* (Director)
1966 *A Man for All Seasons* (Director)
1966 *A Man for All Seasons* (Best Picture)

Directors Guild of America Awards

1954 *From Here to Eternity*
1966 *A Man for All Seasons*
1970 *D.W. Griffith Award*

Directors Guild Nominations

1948 *The Search*
1952 *High Noon*
1957 *A Hatful of Rain*
1959 *The Nun's Story*
1960 *The Sundowners*
1977 *Julia*

Producers' Guild

1966 *Producer of the Year*
     A Man for All Seasons

Golden Globe Awards

1954 *From Here to Eternity* (Best Director)
1966 *A Man for All Seasons* (Best Director)
1966 *A Man for All Seasons* (Best Picture)

Golden Thistle Award

1965 *Edinburgh*

Award City of Vienna

1966 *Gold Medal*

Awards from Moscow

1967 *A Man for All Seasons* (Best Director)
1967 *A Man for All Seasons* (Best Picture)

British Film Academy Awards—London

1967 *A Man for All Seasons* (Best Director)
1967 *A Man for All Seasons* (Best Picture)
Fellowship Award

Christopher Award

1977 *Julia*

Silver Spurs Award—Reno

1953 *High Noon*

Page One Award—New York

1953 *High Noon*

International Office Catholic Cinema

1968 *A Man for All Seasons*

Cinéma Français—Victoire

1952 *High Noon*
1955 *Tant Qu'il Aura des Hommes*

Awards—Seventeen Magazine

1959 *The Nun's Story*
1961 *The Sundowners*
1967 *A Man for All Seasons*

Parents Magazine

1966 *A Man for All Seasons*

Scholastics Magazine Bell Ringer Awards

1967 *A Man for All Seasons*
1977 *Julia*

Box Office Magazine

1944 *The Seventh Cross* (Best Picture of the Month)

Exhibitors Laurel Awards

1948–1953 *High Noon* (Best Action Drama in 5 years)
1952–1953 *High Noon* (Best Feature of the Year)
1953 *From Here to Eternity* (Best Drama)
1957 No. 1 Motion Picture Director
1959 Best Director
1961 Best Director
1966 Top Ten Director
1967 Top Five Director

French Ministry of Culture

1983 Order of Arts and Letters

Berlin Film Festival

1996 Lifetime Achievement Award

Select Bibliography

Archibald, Lewis. "An Interview with Fred Zinnemann." *New York Arts Weekly*, 24 November–1 December, 1982, pp. 34–35.
Astor, Mary. *A Life on Film*, London: W.H. Allen, 1973.
Buckley, Michael. "Fred Zinnemann," *Films in Review*, Volume 34, No. 1, January 1983, pp. 25–40.
Drummond, Phillip. *High Noon*. London: British Film Institute Publishing, 1997.
Finler, Joel. *All Time Box-Office Hits* (General Editor: Neil Sinyard). London: Multimedia Publications, 1985.
Foreman, Carl. "Dialogue on Film." *American Film*, April 1979, pp. 38–39.
_____. "*High Noon* revisited." *Punch*, 25 April, 1972, pp. 448–50.
_____. "Virtue and a Fast Gun," *Observer Magazine*, 10 October, 1965, pp. 21–26.
Foster, Gwendolyn. "The Women in *High Noon*: A Metanarrative of Difference," *Film Criticism*, Spring–Fall, 1994, pp. 72–81.
Giannetti, Louis D. "Fred Zinnemann's *High Noon*," *Film Criticism*, Winter 1976–77, pp. 3–12.
_____. *Masters of the American Cinema*, Eaglewood Cliffs, N.J.: Prentice Hall, 1981.
_____. "The Member of the Wedding." *Literature/Film Quarterly*, Winter 1976, pp. 26–38.
Girgus, Sam B.. *Hollywood Renaissance: The Cinema of Democracy in the Era of Ford, Capra and Kazan*. New York: Cambridge University Press, 1998.
Goldau, Antje; Prinzler Hans Helmut; and Sinyard, Neil. *Zinnemann*. Berlin: Verlag Filmland Presse, 1986.

Gow, Gordon. *Hollywood in the Fifties*. New York: A.S. Barnes, 1971.
_____. "Individualism against Machinery: Interview with Fred Zinnemann."' *Films and Filming*, February 1978, pp. 12–17.
Griffith, Richard. *Fred Zinnemann* (pamphlet). New York: Museum of Modern Art, 1958.
Horton, Robert. "Fred Zinnemann: Day of the Craftsman." *Film Comment*, September–October 1997, pp. 60–67.
Kroll, Jack. "Zinnemann's Climb to the Peak." *Newsweek*, 22 November, 1982, p. 117.
Mayersberg, Paul. *Hollywood the Haunted House*. London: Allan Lane, 1967.
Mayes, Wendell. "Writing for the Movies." *Focus on Film*, No. 7, Summer 1971, p. 41.
McNab, Geoffrey. *Rebel Males*. London: Hamish Hamilton, 1991.
Neve, Brian. "A Past Master of His Craft: An Interview with Fred Zinnemann," *Cineaste*, Volume 23, No. 1, 1997, pp. 15–19.
Nolletti, Arthur (ed.). *The Films of Fred Zinnemann: Critical Perspectives*. New York: State University of New York Press, 1999.
Palmer, Christopher. *The Composer in Hollywood*. London: Marion Boyars, 1976.
Philips, Gene D. "A Conversation with Fred Zinnemann." *Focus on Film*, Spring 1973, pp. 21–34.
_____. "Fred Zinnemann: An Interview," *Journal of Popular Film and Television*, Volume 7, No. 1, 1978, pp. 56–66.
_____. *The Movie Makers: Artists in an Industry*. Chicago: Nelson Hall, 1973.
Rapf, Joanna E. "Myth, Ideology and Feminism in *High Noon*." *Journal of Popular Culture*, Volume 23, No. 4, Spring 1990, pp. 75–80.
Reid, John Howard. "A Man for All Movies: The Films of Fred Zinnemann." *Films and Filming*, May 1967, pp. 5–11.
Sarris, Andrew. *The American Cinema: Directors and Directions*. New York: E.P. Dutton, 1968.
_____. "The Case for Fred Zinnemann." The *Village Voice*, 16 November 1982, pp. 55, 122.
Sinyard, Neil. "Character Is Destiny: A Tribute to Fred Zinnemann." *The National Film Theatre Booklet*, March 1992, pp. 16–17.
_____. *Children in the Movies*. London: Batsford, 1992.
_____. *Classic Movies*. London: Hamlyn, 1985.
_____. *Directors: The All Time Greats*. London: Gallery Books, 1985.
Spoto, Donald. *Stanley Kramer: Filmmaker*. New York: Putnam, 1978.
Stanbrook, Alan. "A Man for All Movies: The Films of Fred Zinnemann."' *Films and Filming*, June 1967, pp. 11–15.
Tobin, Yann. "Zinnemann, première époque." *Positif*, March 1983, pp. 33–34.
Ustinov, Peter. *Dear Me*. London: Heinemann, 1979.
Vidor, King. *On Filmmaking*. London & New York: W.H. Allen, 1973.
Vitoux, Frédéric. "Fred Zinnemann and *Five Days One Summer*." *Positif*, March 1983, pp. 35–37.

Wood, Michael. *America in the Movies*. London: Secker and Warburg, 1975.
Wright, Basil. *The Long View*. London: Secker & Warburg, 1974.
Zinnemann, Fred. "Choreography of a Gunfight." *Sight and Sound*, July–September 1952, pp. 16–17.
_____. *A Life in the Movies: An Autobiography*. New York: Scribner's, 1992.
_____. "Remembering Robert Flaherty." *Action*, May–June 1976, pp. 24–27.
_____. "Revelations." *Films and Filming*, September 1964, pp. 5–6.
_____. "The Story of *The Search*." Hollywood Directors, 1941–1976, edited by Richard Koszarski. Oxford: Oxford University Press, 1977, pp. 143.7.
_____. "Zinnemann Dossier." *Sight and Sound*, Volume 6, No. 1, January 1996.

Index

Abelard and Heloise 133
Act of Violence 24, 37, 38–45, 46, 56, 63, 68, 112, 161
Adler, Buddy 71, 73, 110
Adventures in the Screen Trade 165
All Quiet on the Western Front 11, 134
Allenberg, Bert 73
Anderson, Michael, Jr. 117, 120
Anderson, Robert 82, 86, 166
Angeletti, Marietto 127
Angeli, Pier 54
Arnold, Edward 23
The Ash-Can Fleet 18
Ashcroft, Peggy 84
Astor, Mary 43, 161
Attenborough, Richard 169
Austin, Michael 152

Baby Doll 100
Bach, Johann Sebastian 167
Badal, Jean 129
The Battle of Algiers 136
Battleship Potemkin 9, 15
Becket 90
Beethoven, Ludwig van 167

Behold a Pale Horse 24, 37, 43, 53, 91, 123–132, 137, 147
The Bell Jar 32
Benedek, Laszlo 124
Benjy 51, 59
Bergman, Ingrid 52
Berkeley, Busby 14, 105
Bernstein, Elmer 111, 158
The Best Little Whorehouse in Texas 157
The Best Years of Our Lives 34, 47
The Big Heat 38
The Big Parade 9, 159
Bishop, Richard 57
Black Narcissus 87
Body and Soul 34, 52
Bogart, Humphrey 83
Bolt, Robert 5, 90, 91, 93
Bonney, Therese 31
Bonnot, Alain 5, 133, 146
Borgnine, Ernest 76
Bowman, Lee 21
Box, John 92
Boyle, Kay 27
Brahms, Johannes 167
Brando, Marlon 2, 33, 46, 47, 48, 49, 50, 52

Index

Brantley, Betsy 152, 155, 157
Brecht, Bertolt 24, 93
Bresson, Robert 165
Brown, Clarence 29
Brown, Joe 157
Bruckner, Anton 83
Bus Stop 111
Butler, Ivan 92

Camino Real 73
Capra, Frank 34
Carne, Marcel 162
Chabrol, Claude 136
Champion 46, 50
Chariots of Fire 4
Chertok, Jack 16, 20
The Children's Hour 143
Clayton, Jack 167
Cleary, Jon 116, 117, 118, 166
Clement, Rene 162
Clift, Montgomery 2, 33, 35, 53, 70, 74, 78, 79, 80
The Clock 28
Clouzot, Henri-Georges 162
Cohn, Harry 13, 70, 71, 72, 73, 74, 75
Collinge, Patricia 55
Connery, Sean 2, 152, 153, 154, 155
The Conversation 141
Cooper, Gary 2, 62, 63, 64, 83, 116, 164
Coppola, Francis Ford 141
Corey, Wendell 34
Crawford, Joan 73
Crime Does Not Pay 17, 19
Cronyn, Hume 23, 24
Crosby, Floyd 62, 66
Crossfire 34
Cusack, Cyril 138, 140
Custer 169

Darling 90
Dassin, Jules 17
Davis, Carl 158
The Day of the Jackal 37, 56, 87, 124, 132–140, 167, 168
The Deadly Affair 136
Dean, James 54, 106
Delerue, Georges 135

De Mille, Agnes 107, 108
De Mille, Cecil B. 68, 69
Desert Island Discs 167
De Wilde, Brandon 100, 101, 102
Dietrich, Marlene 10, 76
Double Indemnity 21, 38
Dreyer, Carl 9, 87, 165
Dunnock, Mildred 85
Dyhrenfurth, Norman 157

Edwards, James 104
Eisenstein, Sergei 9, 15
Erdman, Richard 52
Ericson, John 54
Evans, Edith 82, 84
Eyes in the Night 18, 22, 23

Far from the Madding Crowd 108
Finch, Peter 87
Five Days One Summer 1, 2, 13, 53, 57, 100, 103, 110, 136, 147, 148, 149, 151–159, 163
Flaherty, Robert 11–14, 62
Fleming, Victor 29
Fonda, Henry 83
Fonda, Jane 2, 141, 144, 146, 147, 148
Forbidden Passage 19
Ford, John 20, 34, 64, 69, 73, 76, 77, 121
Foreman, Carl 46, 61, 66, 163
Forgotten, Victory 18
Forsyth, Frederick 132
Fort Apache 77
Fox, Edward 132, 134, 140, 162
Franciosa, Anthony 11, 112, 115
Frankenheimer, John 158, 162
Frankenstein 24
French, Philip 168
The French Lieutenant's Woman 12
Friend Indeed 18, 23
From Here to Eternity 2, 5, 6, 7, 37, 50, 51, 67, 69–79, 82, 86, 87, 91, 99, 103, 104, 106, 148, 164, 169
Frost, George 84
Frost, Robert 151
Furtwangler, Wilhelm 24, 168
Fury 24

Index

Gardner, Ava 73
Garland, Judy 28
Garner, Peggy Ann 57
Gazzara, Ben 111
Gazzo, Michael Vincent 110
Gentleman's Agreement 34
Georges-Piquot, Olga 138
Giannetti, Louis D. 162
Glenville, Peter 90
The Go-Between 132
The Godfather: Part II 110
Goethe, Johann Wolfgang 1
Goldman, William 165
Goldstone, Richard 16
Grady, Billy 30
Grant, Cary 83
Graves, Robert 152
Greed 9
La Guerre Est Finie 126
The Guns of Navarone 125

Hallelujah 17
Halliwell, David 92
Hamlet 142
Hammerstein, Oscar 106, 107, 110
Hardy, Thomas 108, 110
Harris, Julie 33, 100, 101, 102, 105
Harrison, Rex 83
A Hatful of Rain 51, 90, 91, 110–115, 147, 166
Hawaii 12, 169
Hawks, Howard 33, 168
Hayes, Alfred 53
Heflin, Van 21, 38, 41, 63
Hellman, Lillian 141
Hendrickson, Floyd 29
Hepburn, Audrey 2, 81, 82, 88, 89
Hepburn, Katharine 142
Herrmann, Bernard 111
Heston, Charlton 91
High Noon 2, 6, 23, 24, 44, 49, 51, 56, 57, 61–69, 71, 79, 86, 91, 100, 106, 110, 130, 135, 137, 147–148, 163, 164
Hilary, Jennifer 157
Hildyard, Jack 121
Hiller, Wendy 91, 169
Hitchcock, Alfred 116, 164, 168
Holbrook, Hal 144
Holden, William 79

Holt, Willy 157
Homage to Catalonia 19
Home of the Brave 34, 46
Houston, Penelope 162
How the West Was Won 76
Hulme, Kathryn 81
Hurt, John 33, 92, 162
The Hustler 10
Huston, John 2, 34, 162, 163, 169

Ibsen, Henrik 6, 153, 159
The Irishman 118
Ivens, Joris 62

Jandl, Ivan 32
Jarre, Maurice 125, 129
Jaws 149
The Jazz Singer 10
John, Errol 88
Johnny Eager 21
Johns, Glynis 117
Johnson, Van 27
Jones, James 69, 70
Jones, Shirley 106, 109
Joyce, James 108
Juggernaut 136
Jurado, Katy 65, 66
Julia 2, 6, 25, 33, 43, 52, 53, 57, 100, 103, 124, 140–149

Kael, Pauline 162
Kaper, Bronislau 38
Kazan, Elia 51, 73, 11, 162
Kelly, Gene 27
Kelly, Grace 65, 66
Kemplen, Ralph 135
Kerr, Deborah 70, 72, 73, 74, 75, 117, 120, 162
The Kid from Spain 14, 105
Kid Glove Killer 21, 22
The King and I 107
The Knack 90
Kramer 46, 47, 50, 61, 66, 71, 99, 100, 162, 163, 164
Kurtz, Gary 1, 5

The Lady or the Tiger? 18, 19
Laemmle, Carl 11
Lamb, Charles 39
Lambert, Diana 89

Lancaster, Burt 5, 70, 72, 75, 77
Lang, Fritz 3, 24, 42, 44
Lastfogel, Abe 46
Lawley 167
Lawrence of Arabia 125
Lean, David 162, 163, 168
Leigh, Janet 38, 41
Lennart, Isobel 118
Lester, Richard 90, 136
The Line-Up 112
Little Mister Jim 29
Loew, Arthur 29, 53
Lonsdale, Michel 130, 139
Look Back in Anger 127
The Looking Glass War 136
Lorentz, Pare 62
Lorre, Peter 42
Losey, Joseph 126, 132
Love Among the Ruins 142
Lubitsch, Ernst 3

M 24, 42
MacInnes, Hamish 2
MacMahon, Aline 32, 33
MacRae, Gordon 106, 109
Macready, George 26
Mahler, Gustav 4, 167
A Man for All Seasons 2, 4, 5, 6, 24, 33, 51, 56, 68, 79, 86, 89–97, 126, 127, 133, 148, 168, 169
Man of Aran 12
The Man Who Shot Liberty Valance 63
Mankiewicz, Joseph L. 68, 69, 76, 81, 101, 162
Mann, Anthony 62
Man's Fate 6, 162
Mayer, Louis B. 13, 20
Mayersberg, Paul 169
Mayes, Wendell 169
McCullers, Carson 99
McGilligan, Patrick 167
McKern, Leo 91
Meeker, Ralph 54
The Member of the Wedding 33, 49, 51, 57, 90, 91, 99–105, 118, 147, 148, 163, 168
The Men 45–52, 54, 55, 113
Menschen am Sontag 10
Mephisto 27

Mifune, Toshiro 169
Milestone, Lewis 11, 134
Miller, David 17
Milton, John 23
Minnelli, Vincente 28
Mitchell, Thomas 69
Mitchum, Robert 2, 116, 117, 120
Mogambo 73
Monkey on My Back 111
Monroe, Marilyn 111
Moorehead, Agnes 24
Mother 15
Murch, Walter 141, 162
Muriel, Gomez 15
Murnau, F.W. 3, 11, 62
Murphy, Rosemary 144
Murray, Don 111, 112, 113

Nada 136
Newman, Paul 59, 106
Nolan, Lloyd 111, 115
Nolletti, Arthur, Jr. 2
North, Alex 104
Novotna, Jarmila 33
The Nun's Story 2, 6, 12, 13, 52, 57, 67, 79, 80–89, 91, 97, 147, 148, 159, 166

O'Casey, Sean 100
The Old South 18
On the Waterfront 95, 111
One Against the World 18
Ophuls, Max 3
Orwell, George 19
Osborne, John 127

Pabst, G.W. 3
The Passion of Joan of Arc 9, 87
Pearl Harbor 169
Peck, Gregory 125, 127, 131
Pellegrin, Raymond 128
Pentimento 141
Planer, Franz 85
Plath, Sylvia 32, 146
Poe, Edgar Allan 65
Pollack, Sydney 141
Pontecorvo, Gillo 136
Potter, Dennis 7
Powell, Michael 87
Power and the Land 62

Index

Preminger, Otto 3
Pressburger 87, 124
Pudovkin, Vsevolod 15

Que Viva Mexico! 15
The Quiet Man 69, 121
Quinn, Anthony 125

Rachel, Rachel 59
Ray, Aldo 72
Rebel Without a Cause 59
Red River 33, 80
Redgrave, Vanessa 96, 130, 141, 144, 147, 162
Reed, Donna 23, 70, 73, 74
Resnais, Alain 126
Ride the High Country 63
Rio Bravo 168
Rio Grande 76
Ritt, Martin 162
The River 62
Roads to the South 126
Robards, Jason 148, 149
Robin and Marian 82
Rodakiewicz, Henwar 14, 15, 16
Rodgers, Richard 106, 107, 110
Roeg, Nicolas 118
Roman Holiday 82
Rome-Open City 47
Room at the Top 167
Rossellini, Roberto 47
Rotunno, Giuseppe 158
Roud, Richard 163
Rowland, Roy 17
Russell, Harold 47
Ryan, Robert 38
Ryan's Daughter 162

Sabrina 82
Saint, Eva Marie 111, 112, 115
Sandburg, Carl 67
Sargent, Alvin 145
Sarris, Andrew 162, 163, 164
Schell, Maximilian 143
Schlesinger, John 90
Schoenberg, Arnold 83
Schweizer, Richard 31, 32
Scofield, Paul 91, 162
The Search 2, 4, 7, 12, 13, 31–38, 43, 46, 52, 53, 57, 80, 100, 112, 141, 142, 168
The Searchers 64
Seghers, Anna 23
The Seventh Cross 2, 23–28, 37, 42, 68, 147, 168
Sharif, Omar 125, 128
Shaughnessy, Mickey 75
Shaw, Robert 91, 96
Shipman, David 167
The Shout 152
Shufftan, Eugene 10
Siegel, Don 112
Silva, Henry 111
Sinatra, Frank 72, 73, 78, 132
Sinden, Donald 134
Siodmak, Robert 3, 10, 44
Sirk, Douglas 114
Skolimowski, Jerzy 152
Sloane, Everett 48, 52
Slocombe, Douglas 142, 162
Smith, Pete 18, 146
Sorel, Jean 138
South Pacific 107
The Spirit of St Louis 106
Spoto, Donald 162
The Spy Who Came In from the Cold 136
Stagecoach 76
Stalag 17 79
Steiger, Rod 33, 54, 106, 107, 108, 109, 130
Stern, Stewart 4, 53, 59
Stevens, George 20, 34, 169
Stevenson, Robert Louis 61
Stoppa, Paolo 129
Strand, Paul 14
Streep, Meryl 33
A Streetcar Named Desire 47
Stroheim, Erich von 3, 9
Stromboli 52
Stuffie 18
Sturges, John 62
The Sundowners 56, 100, 110, 113, 115–121, 148, 166
Szabo, Istvan 27

Tabu 11, 62
Tandy, Jessica 25, 27
Taradash, Daniel 5, 70, 71, 72, 73, 74, 163

Index

Teal, Ray 47
Teresa 24, 33, 49, 52–60, 71, 91, 112, 113, 125, 148, 149, 167
La Terra Trema 15
That Mothers Might Live 17, 18
These Three 16
They Live Again 18
Thomson, David 105
Tiomkin, Dimitri 51, 66, 67, 121
Todd, Mike 105
Toland, Gregg 14, 105
Tournier, Jean 135
Tracking the Sleeping Death 18
Tracy, Spencer 2, 23
The Treasure of the Sierra Madre 121
Truffaut, François 162

Ulmer, Edgar 10
Ustinov, Peter 117, 161, 162

Veigel, Helene 24
Vidor, King 9, 17
Viertel, Berthold 11
Viertel, Peter 33
Visconti, Luchino 15

Walkabout 118
Walker, Alexander 164
Walker, Robert 27
Wallach, Eli 73
Warner, Jack 83, 84
Washington, Ned 67
Waters, Ethel 100, 101, 102
Watson, Wylie 121
The Wave 12, 14–16, 110
Waxman, Franz 83
Weather Wizards 18
Webb, Jack 48, 52
Wechsler, Lazar 29, 31
Welles, Orson 92, 162
When We Dead Awaken 159
While America Sleeps 19
White Shadows in the Seven Seas 13
The Wild Bunch 63
Wilder, Billy 3, 10, 21, 106, 162, 163, 169

Wilke, Robert 78
Williams, Elmo 65, 66, 163
Williams, Tennessee 73
Wilson, Georges 157
Wilson, Lambert 130, 153, 157
Winters, Shelley 111
Wise, Robert 162
Woolf, John 133, 139
Wright, Teresa 46, 47, 48, 49, 52
Written on the Wind 22
Wyler, William 16, 47, 101, 162, 163, 164, 165, 169

York, Susannah 91
Your Last Act 18

Z [film] 97, 136
Zinnemann, Fred: as artist 168; casting against type 74, 106, 132; character as destiny theme 43, 61; children in Z's films 114, 118, 142; documentary instincts and influences 12, 13, 16, 37, 59, 62, 81, 124, 127; dual plot structures in Z's films 37, 42, 43; early experience in Hollywood 10, 11; early life in Vienna 3, 4, 9, 10; endings 19, 84, 130, 159, 169; experiences with MGM and the studio system 5, 6, 16, 20, 21, 28; farewells in Z's films 57, 88; fastidiousness 167; HUAC and McCarthyism 6, 45, 61, 68, 69, 70, 95, 141; hypersensitivity 163; individualism in Z and his films 13, 14, 16, 18, 78, 86, 93; inferiority complex 4; integrity of Z 161, 164; iron will 4, 5, 12, 13, 14, 81, 164, 167; loner heroes 67, 68, 137; parents 3, 4, 168; perfectionism 5; stairwell scenes 24, 25, 57, 115; suspension 28–30; symbolism 56, 65, 66, 159; women in Z's films 147, 148, 149; working with writers 166; *Zivilcourage* 27, 145, 149